IN PRAISE OF *WOMEN OF THE COLORADO MINES*

LINDA WOMMACK'S WONDERFULLY EXCITING NARRATIVE gives great insight into the hardships and rigors of women prospectors in Colorado's rugged mountains. The risks of mining, both physical and financial, were staggering. No wasted words romanticizing daring frontier women's search for gold. Wommack's research and writing are brilliant!

– *New York Times* Bestselling Author, Chris Enss

WOMEN OF THE COLORADO MINES

LINDA WOMMACK

FARCOUNTRY PRESS

ISBN: 978-1-56037-832-7

Design by Steph Lehmann

Cover: Women miners with headlamps. PHOTOGRAPH COURTESY OF LOUISVILLE HISTORICAL MUSEUM.

Back cover, top: Evalyn Walsh McLean with the Hope Diamond in 1914. PHOTOGRAPH COURTESY OF THE LIBRARY OF CONGRESS, LC-USZ62-71454.

Back cover, bottom: Thomas Walsh's Camp Bird Mine. PHOTOGRAPH BY RUSSELL LEE, COURTESY OF THE LIBRARY OF CONGRESS, LC-DIG-FSAC-1A34180.

Chapter heads: Pickaxe. DESIGNED BY MACROVECTOR/FREEPIK

FARCOUNTRY PRESS

For more information about our books, write Farcountry Press, P.O. Box 5630, Helena, MT 59604; call (800) 821-3874; or visit www.farcountrypress.com.

Produced and printed in the United States of America.

29 28 27 26 25 24 1 2 3 4 5 6

CONTENTS

WOMEN WHO SOUGHT THE MOTHER LODE

THE SEARCH FOR THE "MOTHER LODE" has existed on every corner of the earth nearly from the beginning of time. In America, we're all familiar with images of men in dungarees and weather-beaten hats kneeling with a pan in a mountain stream or with a pickaxe slung over their shoulders. Or, better yet, with grunge, grit, and grime from head to toe deep inside a rock cave.

Conversely, there are few images of women in search of the golden riches, but since the Pikes Peak Gold Rush of 1859, women, too, came to the Rocky Mountain

According to her obituary, Ellen "Captain" Jack came to Colorado in the 1870s after her husband died, and she "prospected nearly every mining district... of any note." PHOTOGRAPH COURTESY PIKES PEAK DISTRICT LIBRARY.

West in search of gold. Most, however, made their living supplying the miners' many needs. But a few adventurous, courageous women dug in deep.

These were the women who made a difference in a man's world. They worked their own mines, from Central City's gold diggings to Leadville's silver riches.

The women who mined had a lot of tenacity and gumption. They relied on themselves in order to succeed. Women could do things in the West that weren't allowable according to eastern society. It must have been a liberating feeling. And so they came west and, through determination and hard work, changed the West forever.

When word got out that there was gold in the Pikes Peak region, a grand adventure was begun. It was an exciting yet challenging time. But young people were full of adventure, determined to strike it rich, and so they came.

It was the tough and strong who, through hard work, managed to make a living at this thing called mining. None more so than the women.

The stories of these adventurous gals are stories of strength, courage, humor, and sometimes tragedy. They were female pioneers who made a difference. Their initiative, resourcefulness, and tenacity served them well and also triggered enormous changes, both in the industry and in society.

These women who were stifled in the East found freedom and opportunity in the West.

1

THE RICHEST SQUARE MILE ON EARTH

CENTRAL CITY

PIKES PEAK OR BUST! That was the clarion call to all those seeking their fortune out West. Gold! It had been discovered in the Colorado Rocky Mountains but nowhere near Pikes Peak. No matter. Gold was there for the taking, they said. And so the tinhorns came, by the dozens at first, then by the hundreds, and soon after, by the thousands. And it all started with a friendly competition among a couple of experienced miners from Georgia.

Rumors of gold in the Rocky Mountains had swirled through the wind for centuries. Spaniards such as Coronado (in 1540) and Father Silvestre Vélez de Escalante (in 1776) came in search of elusive riches. They were followed by the French. But it wasn't until prospectors returned from the California Gold Rush of 1849 that any serious attention was paid to the granite slopes of the Rockies.

One such '49er was William Greeneberry Russell. Green, as he liked to be called, hailed from North Georgia where he, like his father, mined the family gold claims for an estimated $20 million. In 1848, Green was chosen to lead a mining expedition to the goldfields of California. Returning to Georgia with plenty of California gold, Green and two of his brothers passed through the Front Range of what would become Colorado. The region looked auspicious to the Green brothers, with promising rivers, creeks, and streams flowing from the high Rocky Mountains onto the plains. And so, in February 1858, the Russell boys—Green, Levi, and Oliver—left their Georgia home in Auraria, Lumpkin County, headed for the Rocky Mountains.

Once Green and his party reached the Santa Fe Trail, they followed the Arkansas River to Bent's Fort (near today's town of La Junta). Fortified with fresh supplies, the group then turned northwest, eventually reaching the confluence of Cherry Creek and the South Platte River on May 23, 1858. Here the men prospected for nearly three weeks without success. They followed the South Platte River upstream to the mouth of Little Dry Creek (approximately where Dartmouth Avenue in Englewood crosses over the South Platte River). Panning for gold at this site, the men managed to wash out nearly $200 in gold (more than $7,000 in today's dollars). It was the first major find along the Front Range, and word of the gold discovery quickly spread.

The Russell brothers set up a placer camp and soon prospectors were arriving from as far away as St. Louis, Missouri, and Lawrence, Kansas. Before the summer was over, however, the gold had played out and the Russell brothers moved downstream to make camp for the winter.

On the east side of the South Platte River and along the banks of Cherry Creek, the Russell group formed the first white settlement at the base of the Front Range. They called it "Auraria" after their hometown in Georgia.[1]

Soon, newspapers far and wide carried news of the gold found in and around the Rocky Mountains. Someone dubbed it the "Pikes Peak Gold Rush," and indeed the rush was on.

John H. Gregory was another Georgian who heard the clarion call—gold! He arrived in the region in January 1859. First prospecting the Cache la Poudre near present-day Fort Collins, Gregory moved south, exploring the creeks along the way. In February 1859, he had made his way upstream in Clear Creek Canyon. Gregory saw good traces of color in a tributary and followed that creek, which would later bear his name. As sometimes happens in gold legends, Gregory looked up at a rock ledge above the creek just as the sun hit at the right angle. Gold glistened in the bright sunlight. Gregory instinctively knew his find was a rich one and that it was far richer than his competitor, Green Russell's, find. He was sure of it. It was May 6, 1859, when Gregory staked two claims on what became known as the Gregory Lode. Today the spot is marked with a plaque about halfway between Central City and Black Hawk in Gregory Gulch. John Gregory later wrote about the experience:

> We all started up Clear Creek prospecting. Arrived in this vicinity May 6th; the ice and snow prevented us from prospecting far below the surface, but the first pan of surface dirt, on the original Gregory claim yielded $4. Encouraged by this success, we all staked out claims, found the "lead" consisting of burnt quartz, resembling the Georgia mines, in which I had

> previously worked. Snow and ice prevented the regular working of the lead till May 16th. From then until the 23rd, I worked it five days with two hands, result $972. Soon after, I sold my two claims for $21,000. Since That time I have been prospecting for other parties at about $200 per day.[2]

William Newton Byers, who had just recently arrived in the Front Range on account of the Pikes Peak or Bust craze, established the first newspaper in the region. He called it *The Rocky Mountain News*. Through his paper, Byers became the region's promoter by writing about events and opportunity. He was the first to hail Gregory's discovery, just as he had Russell's the previous fall. Byers made his first trip up the gulch and reported his experience in the May 28, 1859, edition of his newspaper:

> Crossing the mountains to the Northward we next reach Quartz Creek a tributary of the North Fork of Vasquez River. Near the mouth of this stream the first vein of gold bearing quartz was discovered by J. H. Gregory, of Georgia, on the 6th of May, and much credit is due him for persevering under difficulties having to encounter snow and subsist on what he could shoot with his rifle for two weeks. The vein or lead runs N.N.E. to S.S.W., crossing the creek and extending an unknown distance into the mountains, it has been traced but a short distance.

Until that time, the average gold discovery was worth between $16 and $20 an ounce. With Gregory's discovery far exceeding that, the area became known as "The Richest Square Mile on Earth."

A few weeks later, Byers returned to Gregory Gulch to get a firsthand look at the progress of the goldfield. At that time there were a total of fourteen placer mining claims. Byers set up camp at a section of the gulch that split, one side rock, the other a nice willow grove. As this was a halfway point between the Gregory Diggings and a new camp called Nevada City, Byers suggested to the men that they start a new town: Central City. And so it was.

True to his word, Byers reported Gregory's success in all its gold glory in the June 11 edition of his *Rocky Mountain News:*

> When we entered the diggings on the 20th of May, there were about twenty men in that vicinity, only two Quartz leads had been opened and but three claims on one of those and two on the other. In two weeks from that

> time more than 3,000 men were at work at least thirty leads satisfactorily prospected, and several hundred claims opened and profitably worked. Hundreds of other claims are being opened and new leads are daily discovered. As yet the discoveries and mines are confined to a very small space of country. We think not a claim has been opened outside of a circular tract having a diameter of five miles but the area is steadily increasing and no limit has been found on either side.

Within a month of Gregory's discovery, some 10,000 would-be miners clamored up Clear Creek Canyon to Gregory Gulch. Sluice boxes for separating the gravel and ore were set up all along both sides of the creek.

Gregory carefully chose a few men to help him draw up a few mining rules and regulations. Among the men chosen were Doctor D. Joseph Casto and Charlie Ziegler. Fifteen men made up the group, which became the Gold Miners Association of Gregory District. A meeting of all the miners in the district was then held. *The Rocky Mountain News* reported the event on June 8, 1859:

> Between 2,000 and 3,000 miners turned out for the meeting. Horace Greeley was the first speaker of the day and warned of the temptations of drinking, gambling, etc. He also advocated formation of a new State [*sic*] that might be brought into the Union without going through Territorial status. Several other speakers told of the potential for the area and congratulated the miners on the work so far accomplished. Dr. J. Casto, one of Gregory's original party, urged those miners who had not found paying leads to push on toward the snowy range, where an exploring party was going in a few days. The meeting then adjourned. It was a stirring sight to see so large an assembly in the Mountains and was no doubt surprising to the grizzly bears, who held undisputed sway there six weeks ago.

Among the many rules was "right of discovery." The association held that no miner could hold by right of discovery more than one creek, one gulch, and one mountain claim unless he was the discoverer of the district. This allowed for Gregory to own both of his claims. Each claim had to be worked within ten days to establish ownership. A claim was 100 feet long and 50 feet wide. When applied to a gulch, the footage extended bank to bank. Placer mines were 100 feet square. Water rights were adjusted to no more than 200 feet. If disputes arose, a jury of three settled the matter.

These rules and regulations, the first in the region, became the foundation for all mining districts in Colorado.

Meanwhile, Gregory's old Georgia friend and rival, Green Russell, heard about the Gregory Diggings and didn't want to be left out. He headed to the hills with a small party and in no time at all hit pay dirt, four miles south of Gregory Gulch in an area now known as Russell Gulch. Russell quickly realized the need for good drinking water and helped his friend Gregory develop the gold region by establishing the Consolidated Ditch Company in Russell Gulch. Finally, the Georgia rivals, Russell and Gregory, were working together—and they were getting rich! Russell wrote a letter detailing his discovery on June 17, 1859.

> The prospects in the veins or mountain diggings, as they call call them here, is improving. There are now about 75 sluices in operation, all washing the ore taken from the veins, which is paying variously from $5 to $50 per day to the hand. There is a company of five men working within 200 yards of this place, on vein which they lately discovered, and yesterday they carried the ore to the branch, washed it in a common box sluice, and made $125; and today they have taken $5 out of a single pan of ore.

The frenzy of swarming prospectors and rich gold discoveries was now exciting national news as evidenced in a *New York Tribune* article written by reporter Horace Greeley, who was visiting the Gregory Diggings:

> Six weeks ago, this ravine was solitude, the favorite haunt of elk, the deer, and other shy denizens of the profoundest wilderness, seldom invaded by the footsteps of the man. Now, anyone who has been here for three weeks is considered an old-timer.[3]

And this from *The Rocky Mountain News* on June 18, 1859:

> Since our last issue we have again spent several days in the Gregory Diggings and vicinity. Every day witnesses new gold-digging discoveries and the mines already opened grow richer as they descend. The amount of gold obtained from some of them seems almost incredible. The idea that pan after pan and wagon load after wagon load of dirt can be taken from a mine that will pay ten, or even five, dollars to the pan seems beyond belief, but it is nevertheless true.

The July 4 edition contained the following:

> There are at present about 10,000 men at the mines, of that number perhaps 500 are making money, the greater portion, however, are not making expenses. Times here at present are dull, the merchants and traders get all the dust, and take it to the States, and persons cannot afford to improve the place yet.

The same paper gave an estimate of the gold riches on December 21, 1859, reporting that "from a million and a half to two million of dollars in dust has been taken out, which has found its way to all parts of the Atlantic States and Territories." And then from the same publication dated February 6, 1860:

> The Big Nugget - Quite a stir was created last week by the report of the discovery of a six pound nugget near Gregory's. It was said to have "but little quartz about it." Some of our heavy merchants sent immediately to purchase it, offering $16 per ounce in coin—came back with fleas in their ears. Our sprightly little neighbor the "Mountaineer," gave the names of the fortunate finders, and valued the "chunk" at "over twelve hundred dollars" but the mother declined to part with "the little darling" for even those fabulous figures —all in coin—and the value of the "big lumps" has materially depreciated among bachelor speculators. How is it gentlemen?

In the June 18, 1860, edition of *The Rocky Mountain News,* Byers printed a wonderful ode to the new gold discoveries of the Rocky Mountain region.

We expect hard times, we expect hard fare,
Sometimes sleep in the open air;
We'll lay on the ground and sleep very sound,
Except when Indians are howling around.

CHORUS:
Then ho boys ho, to Cherry Creek we'll go.
There's plenty of gold
In the West, we are told,
In the new Eldorado.

We'll rock our cradles around Pikes Peak
In search of the dust, and for nuggets
we seek;

If the Indians ask us why we are there,
We'll tell them we're made as free as the air.

The gold is there, 'most anyway.
You can take it out rich with an iron
crowbar,
And where it is thick, with a shovel and pick
You can pick it out in lumps as big as a
brick.

If the dirt don't pay,
We can strike our tents most any day.
We know we are bound to strike a streak
Of very rich quartz among the
mountain peaks.

Oh dear girls, now don't you cry,
We are coming back by and by;
Don't you fret nor shed a tear,
Be patient wait about one year.

But not all the "girls" were patient. Some were just as eager, just as determined as their male counterparts to strike their own fortunes in gold.

Colorado's Rags to Riches Story: Elizabeth "Baby Doe" McCourt Doe

The year 1877 dawned bright and clear for Elizabeth Nellis Bonduel McCourt Doe. She had arrived in the "Richest Square Mile on Earth." She and her husband, W. H. Doe Jr., intended to make their fortune from the Fourth of July Mine high above Central City. Little did Elizabeth know that her fortune lay far in the future and far away. Not from Central City gold, but from Leadville silver.

Born in 1854 in Oshkosh, Wisconsin, Elizabeth was the fifth of fourteen children of Irish Catholic parents, Peter and Elizabeth McCourt. In the celebrated St. Peter's Roman Catholic Church, she was christened "Elizabeth Nellis McCourt," Nellis being her mother's maiden name. Later, Lizzie, as she was called in her formative years, would add the name "Bonduel" after the city's beloved Father Florimond Bonduel, a dear friend of the McCourt family. It was the first of many embellishments she created throughout her lifetime, fudging her age by six to eight years being one of them.

As the daughter of well-to-do parents, Lizzie was a precocious child, which served her well in gaining friends at an early age. As a teenager she became a bit stand-offish with other girls her age, but she was charming and loved to flirt with the boys. It was no surprise to Lizzie when she became known to all as the "Belle of Oshkosh."

Tragedy struck the town of Oshkosh in 1874 when fire broke out. Lizzie's father lost his business as well as the family home. Then, just as Peter McCourt was finishing his rebuilding, fire broke out again on April 28, 1875. The town was decimated and the McCourt family faced financial ruin. It would not be the last time young Lizzie would lose everything.

In the summer of 1875, twenty-year-old Lizzie spent the long, hot days clerking for her father in his new trailer shop. One particularly warm afternoon, a young man approximately her age walked into the store. They seemed to lock eyes on one another as he introduced himself. He was William "Harvey" Doe Jr., the son of one of the most influential families in Oshkosh. Soon young Mr. Doe came to call on Lizzie at the McCourt home. Recalling the time years later, Lizzie said, "He would come over to play the piano for all my family in the evening, seeming to love us all. He would join in the general fun without trying to monopolize me, like other men."[4]

By summer's end they were in love. The prosperous German Protestant Does were not happy with their son's choice in love, particularly his mother. On the other hand, the once wealthy Irish Catholic McCourts were in favor of their daughter's choice for financial reasons rather than religious ideology.

That winter the Congregational Church, to which the Doe family belonged, sponsored an ice skating contest to raise funds for youth activities. Harvey Doe intended to compete for the top prize. Ever eager to be the center of attention, Lizzie let it be known she would enter the competition as well. No matter that she would be the only girl to skate, Lizzie was nothing if not determined. Oh, how the tongues must have wagged in Oshkosh!

On the day of the competition, Lizzie was indeed the center of attention when she skated onto the ice of frozen Lake Winnebago. Blonde-haired, blue-eyed Lizzie McCourt skated with perfection, performing figure eights, twirls, and arabesques flawlessly, requiring the necessary but unladylike showing of bare legs. Naturally, for she had no doubt the outcome, Lizzie won the competition—proving she was indeed the belle of Oshkosh. This young woman's "world-be-damned" attitude never waivered for the remainder of her years.

Finally, when Lizzie and Harvey announced their plans for marriage, both sets of parents eventually acquiesced to the idea. Lizzie was once again the center of attention as she and her mother prepared her trousseau. Not to be outdone, William H. Doe Sr. announced that he would offer his Colorado mine to the bride and groom as a wedding gift.

Lizzie must have been beside herself. Not only would her wedding be the finest in all of Oshkosh, but she and Harvey would soon be rich with Colorado gold.

The wedding of Elizabeth Nellis Bonduel McCourt and William Harvey Doe Jr. took place at St. Peter's Catholic Church on June 27, 1877. The bride was twenty-two years old and the groom was twenty-three. Immediately following the wedding, the bride and groom were ushered to the train station. It was Lizzie's first train trip—a honeymoon to the rich goldfields of Colorado. Arriving in Denver, the newlyweds spent nearly two weeks at the American House before their next journey, to the gold mines of Central City.

Elizabeth McCourt Doe came to Colorado with her husband, William H. Doe Jr., seeking their fortunes in mining.
PHOTOGRAPH BY ALFRED E. RINEHART, COURTESY OF DENVER PUBLIC LIBRARY, SPECIAL COLLECTIONS.

The newlyweds were excited to see their new gold mine, especially Lizzie. The couple arrived in the mining town of Black Hawk on the Colorado Central Railroad, a narrow gauge train that allowed easier navigation through the narrow canyons. As the railroad had not yet reached Central City, Lizzie and Harvey traveled the one mile up Gregory Gulch, a steep 500-foot trip uphill, by stagecoach. The stage passed the mining camps of Mountain City, Dogtown, and Nevadaville, all cramped into that mile of gulch between the two major towns. Wasting no time, the couple hurried to their mine the following day.

The Fourth of July Mine was located just south of the mining town, on Quartz Hill. The mine was an investment made by Harvey's father and his partner, Benoni C. Waterman, purchased on August 24, 1871.[5] The Economic Geology for the Central City District described the mine as follows:

> **Fourth of July Mine** (C-IV-35)
>
> Location—On the northeast slope of Quartz Hill about 1,370 feet S. West of Quartz Hill tunnel.
>
> Production—18.68 ounces of gold
>
> Vein—steep on either side of vertical 6 to 10 inches wide. Cross fracture in places
>
> Ore and mineral—pyrite, gold, white and dark gray quartz
>
> Ore shoots—Shaft is in center of main shoot that plunges to the west and has a stope length of 150 feet[6]

Despite the moniker "Richest Square Mile on Earth," the mine had not produced for the partners. Therefore, when W. H. Doe's son announced his engagement, Doe offered to buy out Waterman. A deal was reached in which Doe would lease the mine, paying Waterman $10,000 the first year and $15,000 the second year. Doe's plan was to sink a shaft 200 feet where he was sure he would hit pay dirt.

All of this was contingent, of course, on Harvey Doe Jr.'s due diligence in working and managing the mine. If successful, the profits and eventually the deed would be owned by Harvey and Lizzie.

The Does moved into a small cabin just down the hill and at the edge of Central City, on Spring Street. Ironically, Lizzie's first Colorado home, a cabin dwelling, would also be the last type of home for her in Colorado.

It was not long before Lizzie realized she was not cut out to be a housewife. While she kept the cabin neat and clean, she was soon bored with household chores. Lizzie insisted on accompanying her husband when her father-in-law introduced him to various Central City businessmen, including the influential banker Joseph Thatcher of the First National Bank. Lizzie also happened to make the acquaintance of William "Billie" Bush, the proprietor of a fabulous hotel, the Teller House. The meeting proved advantageous in the moment, as well as for future happenings. In any case, while in Central City, Thatcher and Bush became Lizzie's trusted advisors. Intrigued by the business and financial dealings of mining, she set out to learn all she could.

Of the many things Lizzie learned, one was particularly disturbing as it affected her directly. She learned from Mr. Thatcher that her father-in-law had not filed the signed lease agreement between he and his partner with the bank. Without a proper recording, the mine remained in partnership and Harvey's hard work would be for naught. Alarmed by this news, Lizzie hired a horse team and drove directly to the mine to tell her husband, where more bad news awaited her. It was already the first of September and Harvey had yet to begin work on sinking the new shaft. Lizzie now took control of the situation and her future. She and Harvey went to the bank where they had his father's partnership lease agreement recorded and obtained a loan for sinking the second shaft.

With only a few months before winter set in, Lizzie suggested sinking two shafts to double their profits in a hurry. With Lizzie's persuasion, Mr. Thatcher authorized a second loan with the First National Bank. Whether Lizzie instinctively realized her husband was weak or she truly had a desire to work the mine will never be known, but work the mine she did. Every morning she donned men's trousers, a shirt, and boots. She drove the team and Harvey to the mine where she made sure they both put in a full day's work. They each worked with a crew on separate shafts, and Lizzie handled the horse-pulled hoist. She hauled timber for the shafts, dug the dirt, and mucked right alongside the men.

It was unusual for a woman to work a mine—some thought it unladylike, others were superstitious and deemed it bad luck. Nevertheless, Lizzie quickly developed a good working relationship with the miners, and they affectionately bestowed her with the nickname "Baby." Although Harvey hated it, Lizzie must have liked it as it stuck, and everyone called her Baby or Baby Doe from then on.

In October 1877, a reporter for the *Mining Reporter* wrote the following during one of his trips to Gregory Gulch:

> I next reached the Fourth of July lode, a mine which has not been worked for several years, but started some months ago under the personal supervision of the

> owner, Mr. W. H. Doe and his wife. The young lady manages one half of the property while her liege lord manages the other. I found both of their separate shafts managing a number of workmen, Mr. Doe at his which is 70 feet, and his wife, who is full of ambition, in her new enterprise, at hers which is sunk 60 feet. This is the first instance where a lady, and such she is, has managed a mining property. The mine is doing very well and produces some rich ore.

Sinking the two shafts seemed to prove profitable for Harvey and Baby Doe, at least for a time. As the income began to slow, so did Harvey's ambition. He left Baby alone in the evenings while he found better company in the saloons. Soon, even on Sundays, the only day the couple did not work at the mine, Harvey could be found in a Central City saloon. It was left to Baby to manage the mine. Soon she was forced to shut down operations on one of the shafts. As the financial situation grew dire, Harvey wrote his parents to ask for a loan. Unfortunately, Harvey continued to spend more time in the saloons than at the mine.

This obviously showed in the profit and loss statements William Harvey Doe Sr. received. It wasn't long before the family loans were stopped. Harvey and Baby were forced to vacate their log cabin in Central City and move to cheaper accommodations. They found a small apartment on the upper floor of the Rohling Block building on Gregory Street.

Despite the downturn, or because of it, Baby worked even harder at their mine. But little profit was gained for her effort. Her friend and advisor Billie Bush owned both the Lewis and South Lewis mines that adjoined the eastern boundary of the Fourth of July Mine. That fall, Bush's Cornish miners were hoisting rich ore, netting an average of $700 a month. Baby was sure it was just a matter of time before her mine (for she no longer felt she was in partnership with her lackadaisical husband) would be just as rich as Bush's mines were.

Meanwhile, Harvey managed to get a job mucking at the nearby Bobtail Mine. The richest in the district, this mining company boasted three stamp mills for the production of an average of $500,000 annually.

As winter set in, Baby formulated a plan that by springtime she would work her mine even more efficiently than before. She knew that since her husband had given up on the mine, her father-in-law would never give them the deed. With the few profits she managed to make, Baby began buying small claims at $50 each.

It was during this time that Baby and Harvey met Jacob Sandelowsky, whose mercantile, Sandelowsky, Pelton & Company, was just a few doors down from where the Does lived. The trio became fast friends and enjoyed dining together at Jake's invitation or in the Does' apartment.

The following spring, Baby returned to the mine. The next few months brought good profits, but by May very little paying ore was uncovered from nearly all the mines in the gulch. Ironically this was the same time that a bonanza of silver had been discovered in Leadville. It was an event that was not lost on Baby.

The month of May brought changes for Baby and Harvey. Baby learned she was pregnant about the time Harvey lost his job at the Bobtail Mine. He had no choice but to return to working the Fourth of July Mine since Baby could no longer do such hard physical labor. Harvey, however, did not have the management skills his wife possessed and was soon borrowing money from the First National Bank without Baby's knowledge. Then when Harvey Doe Sr. found out about the unpaid loans, he shut down the mine. And just like that Baby lost her dream of getting rich from Colorado gold. Nevertheless, she remained determined—she would find another way.

The Does began to argue, mostly about money. Harvey worked in various mines, but the jobs never lasted and there was never any money. Harvey began to spend more and more time in the saloons.

For only a short time that early summer, due to her condition, Jake Sandelowsky allowed Baby to clerk in his mercantile store. With this income, Baby managed to pay the rent and buy a few groceries. It was during this time that Baby, alone at night, began working on the first of many of her scrapbooks.[7] Later that summer, when Baby went into labor, Harvey was nowhere to be found. It was left to their good friend Sandelowsky to come to Baby's aid.[8] Sadly, on July 13, 1879, Baby's child, a boy, was stillborn. Baby wrote in her scrapbook: "My baby boy had dark, very dark hair, very curly, and large blue eyes."[9]

Her infant son was buried in the Catholic section of the cemetery on the hill above town. The grave was not marked. When she was able, Baby returned to work at Sandelowsky's mercantile. Harvey worked occasionally but spent most of his time in the saloons. Baby began to resent Harvey and regretted her marriage. It must have been a heart-wrenching decision, but despite her Catholicism, Baby asked Harvey for a divorce. He refused. The couple spent a miserable winter arguing.

In January 1880, Baby caught Harvey leaving a house of ill repute. Although she was shocked, she quickly tucked the information away for future reference. Harvey disappeared again, and Baby learned from friends he was in Denver. She also was informed that he frequented a bordello on Market Street owned by Lizzie Preston. Baby put her plan together, and on the night of March 2, 1880, she led police to Lizzie's place and confronted her husband.[10] With the police as her witnesses, Baby would now have the proof she needed for a divorce: adultery.

Lizzie entered the establishment after the police and went from room to room until she found her husband. Just as she suspected, Harvey was in a most compromising situation. The incident was covered the next day in the *Denver Tribune,* most likely due to the scandalous nature of the wife confronting the cheating husband in the very act. It would not be the last scandal Baby would be involved in.

Baby hired the prominent Denver attorney C. W. Wright. The well-known judge, Amos Steck, presided.[11] After the judge heard from the witnesses, he granted Baby her divorce. Baby sold her furniture and her jewelry to pay for the attorney.

Sandelowsky had been planning on opening another store in the new silver boomtown of Leadville. He asked Baby to join him. Down on her luck and looking to make another strike, in silver, if need be, Baby agreed to go to Leadville.

As we'll see in Chapter 3, this was a decision that would change her life. From rags, Baby was about to finally find her riches.

"Angel of the Rockies": Clara Brown

One morning at about five o'clock, a woman was walking up Eureka Gulch, just above where the Methodist Episcopal church now stands, with a basket of clothes on her head, singing as she strode along under her heavy burden. Taking her load down for a moment and seating herself to rest, she began clapping her hands and shouting. "Bless the Lord! Bless the Lord! I am so happy this morning." A prominent lawyer, passing just then, hearing her songs of praise and expressions of joy, said to himself, as he walked on, "What is it that makes that colored woman so happy? She certainly must have something that I have not!" That reflection, after a little, became the means of his conversation.[12]

Clara Brown was a tall, slender woman, about sixty-five years old when she arrived in Colorado, one of the '59ers. Central City sits at an elevation of 8,500 feet, and Eureka Gulch is high above the town, accessed by a steep trail. Imagine walking at that altitude, at that age, with a heavy basket on your head! Her stamina matched her determination, her perseverance, her goodwill, and her loving heart.

Clara Brown was born a slave, lived the life of a slave, and married a slave with whom she had children. Clara was sold to other slave holders, as was her husband, and most tragic of all, she lost her four children to the slave trade. She lost all she loved and lived for, yet she found the strength and courage to go on.

Over the years, many historians and early biographers have had a hard time placing Clara's birth date and location. Many have cited Virginia, Tennessee, or Kentucky, while the year of her birth is stated as anywhere from 1800 to 1806. This is not so unusual, as birth records of slaves were quite rare indeed. Compounding her genealogy is the fact that Clara was the property of a man named Smith, and she was later bought by a man named Brown, which she took as her name upon her freedom. Such common names as Brown and Smith only added twists to the fine thread of unlocking Clara's past.

Clara Brown was highly regarded for her industriousness and generosity. PHOTOGRAPH COURTESY OF DENVER PUBLIC LIBRARY, SPECIAL COLLECTIONS.

Roger Baker, Central City historian, has quite possibly conducted the most comprehensive research on the early life of Clara Brown to date. Among the many facts unearthed by Baker, he lays out the case for each of the claims of birth location and dates, dispelling some claims, while acknowledging that definitive documentation simply does not exist.

The facts at hand seem to lean to Clara's birth year as 1803, in Virginia, possibly in Spotsylvania County near Fredericksburg. Clara herself quite honestly did not know her birth date. In an interview with the *Denver Republican* in 1885, the elderly woman was asked about her age. Responding, she could recall only that she was a "good-sized girl during the War of 1812."

Clara and her mother lived on a Virginia tobacco plantation owned by Ambrose Smith, where they worked primarily as house servants. At the age of eighteen, Clara married another slave at the plantation.[13] Four children were born to this union: Richard, Margaret, and twins, Eliza Jane and Paulina Anna. The first of many tragedies in Clara's remarkable life occurred when Paulina drowned at the age of eight.

When Ambrose Smith died in 1835, liquidation of the Smith estate meant selling property. Clara along with her husband and children were displayed for all to see, one at a time, on the local auction block. Clara must have watched in horrified disbelief as first her husband was sold, then her son, and finally her two daughters. Last on the auction block was Clara. One can only imagine the desperation and humiliation she must have felt.

Clara was heartsick and alone for the first time in her life. Years later, her anguish perhaps dimmed by the passage of time, Clara told a reporter for the *Denver Tribune Republican* in 1885, "My little sufferings was nothing, honey and the Lord He give me the strength to bear up under them, I ain't complaining."

A Kentucky plantation owner and prosperous hat maker, George Brown must have sensed Clara's distress, for he bid high for her and won the bid. For the next twenty-one years, Clara worked as a domestic slave for the Brown family on the plantation. Clara would later recall that there was "always plenty to eat and plenty to wear." She also recalled being beaten, however, "not of'en."

In 1856, upon the death of George Brown, Clara was eventually granted her freedom. While some historians have said it was George Brown who gave Clara her freedom, Roger Baker, Clara's biographer, rejects that claim. His research turned up the will of George Brown, which listed Clara in recorded print for the first time, as receiving $300 from the Brown estate. It was actually the Brown daughters who secured Clara's freedom. In any case, Clara was finally a free woman, and so grateful to her master of those many years she took his surname, Brown, and looked forward to a new beginning, as did many African Americans of the time.

For a host of reasons, some more obvious than others, that new beginning was out West. For Clara, it was an exciting opportunity and a slim chance to find her children. By this time, she had learned that both her husband and daughter Margaret had died. Richard had been sold so many times that Clara had lost track of him, and she had no idea where Eliza Jane was, but she still held out hope of finding them one day.

The Brown family helped Clara receive clear passage as a free citizen to St. Louis, Missouri, where freed slaves were protected by law under the Missouri Compromise of 1854. Here she found employment as a domestic servant with a local family. Within a year's time, Clara pushed on toward her goal of going west. She gained employment in Leavenworth, Kansas, where she kept a sharp eye on those who were moving to the West.

In April 1859, Clara approached a military leader who was escorting a sixty-wagon caravan to the West. She offered to cook for the team of escorts in exchange for her fare and transportation of her possessions, including stoves and washtubs. Clara was allowed to join the group traveling west, but the journey was quite grueling. Throughout the 700-mile journey, Clara walked much of it, alongside the wagon, while cooking and cleaning as best she could during the evening stops and before the journey resumed in the morning. After eight weeks of travel under the hot sun, biting rain, and the ever-constant wind, Clara and her wagon train reached Denver City on June 8, 1859. With this newest arrival, among the many that would become known as the '59ers, Clara Brown became the first African-American woman to reach the Colorado goldfields.

In Denver, Clara rented a one-room log cabin and set up her laundry business in the middle of the thriving little city along the path to gold riches. Through her business, she made friends and business contacts and saved her money. She was one of seven of a nondenominational congregation that met in the cabin of Reverend Jacob Adriance. On November 6, 1859, the group formed the Union Sunday School. Clara donated to charities, helped the sick and poor, and was devoted to the church. It is about this time that Clara became known as the "Angel of the Rockies."

Clara then joined the mad rush of fortune seekers heading up to Gregory Gulch to the new gold strike camp of Central City. On April 1, 1860, Clara negotiated for a ride in a wagon up the steep mountain. Settling in the crude mining camp, Clara secured a three-room cabin where she used one room to operate her laundry business, knowing her services would be needed by the local miners. She built a woodshed where she could store the much-needed firewood for heating water for the laundry. Clara charged fifty cents a bundle, usually twenty items of clothing, for her services. This was at a time when miners made an average of ten dollars a week. To further her income, Clara provided cooking and cleaning services. She was a hard worker, frugal, and in time, Clara accumulated money. She made friends and began to feel a real sense of belonging to a community. She met people who were willing to help her with investments, and she enlisted help from a few black friends she had made in Denver, such as Jeremiah Lee and Lorenzo Bowman. By the end of the Civil War in 1865, Clara had invested in mining claims and real estate in both Denver and Central City, and had saved an estimated $10,000. This was an incredible accomplishment for any sole proprietor in a small mountain mining camp. Of note is an entry in the Gilpin County Record book.[14] Here can be found a recorded deed dated October 1, 1860, in Clara's name. She purchased a lot described as "the 1st lot west of the new one and a half story log house built by Cook and McBride." She paid $50 for the property and sold it in 1868 for $500. A note on the sale reads: "the house built by me 1860." Later, Clara purchased two buildings on the south side of Lawrence Street from Henry Teller for $500. She was so respected as a property owner that Clara was the subject of an editorial in the *Daily Central City Register* issue of March 26, 1873:

> It has frequently been said that this is a great country for the industrious poor to get rich in, and our city is a good illustration of this. By this book we find that Aunt Clara, who, a few years ago, was a slave, (if we mistake not, in Mr. Thatcher's native State,) has, by honest industry at the washtub, accumulated so much property that its assessed value is greater than that of the institution above referred to.[15]

As one of the few African Americans in the small but growing community of Central City, Clara's presence brought comfort to others. She fed the needy, helped the sick, and helped with the birthing of babies. The *Denver Republican* of February 1890 wrote of Clara, "She was always the first to nurse a sick miner or the wife of one, and her deeds of charity were numerous."

So beloved was Clara that after a local citizen had verbally accosted her on the streets of Central City, the *Daily Miner Register* came to her defense. Under the headline "Insulted on Street" in the April 26, 1866, issue, the editor wrote, "There is not a more respectable, upright colored woman in the territory than 'Aunt' Clara, despite some low-life fellow."

It was because of her caring ways and unassuming acts of kindness early on that she had become known as "Aunt" Clara, a respectable title bestowed upon elderly black women. While Clara became endeared in this way, she also saw the importance of living within a strong community. In Central City, her business and her home became a mainstay for the homeless, or sick or injured miners, regardless of race, where Clara gave them a place to recover and cared for them until they were able to return to work. So beloved was she that the August 7, 1866, issue of *The Rocky Mountain News* noted her fine character. Under the headline, "A Woman in a Thousand," the editorial read in part, "We will put 'Aunt' Clara against the world, white or black, for industry, perseverance, energy, and filial love."

Clara's charity went further into the community of Central City, and most likely was an act of true devotion. While in Denver, Clara had forged a close bond with Henry Reitze and the Methodist Church. According to *The Rocky Mountain News,* Clara, along with Reitze, D. W. Collier, and O. F. Goldrich, was among those who met in the cabin of Methodist Reverend Jacob Adriance to form the nondenominational Union Sunday School. The first few meetings were held in Reverend Adriance's home, which had a dirt floor, and one window. A devoted Christian, Clara was one of the first to support the reverend, who had been sent west to establish Methodist missions in Denver and Central City. Clara also contributed to four different churches during her time in Denver.

Aunt Clara continued her charity and devotion in Central City, where she became reunited with her old Denver friend, Reverend Jacob Adriance, who was preaching his sermons in Central City. She helped the reverend start the first Sunday school program in town, offering her home on Lawrence Street as the classroom. She became a leading supporter in the Methodist community, advocating for the need of a church, giving her time and generous monetary contributions toward this cause. The new Methodist congregation met at Clara's home for the first few years until the present church was built. Finally, in February 1863, workers broke ground on Eureka Street for the building of St. James Methodist Church. According to Central City pioneer Henry Hawley, Clara Brown was the largest donor to the effort.

Following the end of the Civil War, Clara felt it was safe to renew her search for the family she had lost. Her literate friends wrote letters for her, sending inquiries into the South. Receiving a few credible tips, Clara used much of her savings and in 1866 traveled to Kentucky and Tennessee in search of her loved ones. While Clara failed to find her daughter Eliza Jane, she was able to gather sixteen of her extended relatives and friends together. She paid their fare to Colorado, where she helped them find employment, many in Central City. *The Rocky Mountain News* issue of August 7, 1866, reported on Clara's first trip east:

> Mrs. Clara Brown, (colored) better known to old Coloradians [*sic*] as "Aunt Clara," came here in '59, and by dint of hard labor and perseverance had amassed quite a fortune. Last October the secret of her economy and industry for all these years came to light, and her object apparent. She at that time went east and has since devoted her time and energies to looking up numerous progeny; for that purpose she traveled through the length and breadth of Kentucky and Tennessee, gathering her flock, and the result is she has now come back to her chosen home in the mountains. She brought them all out at her own expense, arriving last week, and proposes to settle them around her.

Fire was a constant danger in mountain mining towns, and Clara Brown found herself a victim of a blaze in April 1872. The *Central City Register* issue dated April 18, 1872, reported the incident:

> Last evening, about five o'clock, the citizens living in the vicinity of McCall and Lewis' Central Barn, were startled by the cry of fire. Messrs. Giddings, Lewis and Sabin, were in the aforesaid barn at the time, engaged in conversation, when the alarm was given. Hastily picking up buckets and filling them with water, they rushed to the scene, and found that the house on fire belonged to Aunt Clara Brown. Through their united efforts the fire was extinguished. It is supposed to have originated from a defective flue.

The great fire of May 21, 1874, which destroyed so much of Central City, also took three houses owned by Clara.

In 1879, Clara was personally asked by Governor Pitkin to serve as the Colorado representative to visit African-American groups in Kansas, where many black people had escaped from the South and moved to black homesteads. Known in history as the "Exodusters," it was the governor's hope that Clara could convince these folks to come to Colorado for a better opportunity. Due to miner strikes and labor shortages, there were many jobs available in Colorado. Aunt Clara, in her late seventies, accepted the appointment and delivered Governor Pitkin's invitation to the Exodusters of Kansas and even donated some of her own money to support the new black communities formed in Colorado. The September 28, 1879, *Central City Register* later reported on the event:

> Aunt Clara Brown, whom everybody in Central knows, returned from a visit to Kansas some few days since, whither she went to look into the condition of the colored refugees and in the interest of the sufferers generally. There were about 500 all told, and they are getting on as fast as could be expected. The greater portion have found employment, and the balance will, doubtless, in the course of time. Aunt Clara says they are an industrious and sober class of people who only ask an opportunity to make an honest living. Their cry is work, work, and that is being given them as fast as possible She was kindly received by Governor St. John [Kansas] and the people generally. She thinks that in another year these people will be well-to-do and self-supporting.

Clara's health began to suffer due to her age and the high altitude at Central City. She moved to Denver where a friend generously offered Clara a small white frame house on a back lot, rent free for life. It was here that she continued the search for her family with a letter writing campaign. The March 7, 1884, issue of the *Denver Republican* carried the story, reporting, "Misfortune came upon her [Clara] in sundry ways, and she was reduced to poverty having to depend upon those who had known her in other circumstances for aid. Mr. Charles Cheever provided a comfortable home for her at 517 Arapahoe Street."

In March 1884, the letter writing finally yielded a credible lead. Clara, now nearing her eighties, received word that a black woman named Eliza lived in Council Bluffs, Iowa. She was born about the same time as Clara's child, Eliza, and had been taken from her mother and sold to another plantation. Clara, desperate to follow this lead, went to her church and friends, who supplied the travel fare. With clearance from her doctor, Clara went by train to a hopeful reunion in Council Bluffs. There, as Clara rode in a streetcar, she saw a woman walking along a muddy street. Immediately she knew it was her Eliza Jane. Clara stepped off the streetcar and held out her arms to her long lost daughter.

The story of their reunion was published in newspapers in Colorado and throughout the Midwest. The Council Bluffs local paper described Clara as "still strong, vigorous, tall, her hair thickly streaked with gray, her face kind."

Cards and letters of best wishes and congratulations were sent to Clara from all over the country. She contacted the *Denver Republican,* which printed a message of thanks: "Old Aunt Clara, the colored woman so well known in Central and in this city, wishes to express her thanks to the many friends by whose generosity she has been enabled to meet her daughter, who was sold out of her arms at the age of one and a half years, some forty years ago." After more than forty years of separation from her daughter, Clara's dream had finally come true. Eliza Jane was the only child Clara ever found, and the two returned to Colorado where they lived together until Clara's death.

In March 1884, the Society of Colorado Pioneers held a benefit dinner in Clara's honor and inducted her as the first black pioneer of Colorado into the society. The March 7, 1884, issue of the *Denver Republican* reported, "Dressed in a neat calico dress, turban, and white apron, Aunt Clara received her many guests. They included once dead-broke miners she had helped and who had since become affluent."

A year later, Clara gave what would be her last interview. "When did you see your husband last, Aunt Clara?" asked a reporter for the *Denver Tribune Republican* on June 26, 1885. She rocked slowly in her chair and replied, "I don't remember just when. He was sold nearly thirty years ago. I don't know where they took him. I had four children, too, darlin.' They sold them, too."

Clara Brown passed away peacefully in her sleep on October 23, 1885. A reporter for the *Denver Republican* recounted her final moments in the October 27, 1885, issue:

> On the night of her death the scene inside the little cottage on Arapahoe street was solemn and impressive. The room was but dimly lighted, and there was a score of dusky forms seen through the shadows rocking their bodies back and forth in the manner peculiar to their race, and calling on the Lord, in their strange fashion, for his merciful comfort and assistance.
>
> On the bed in one corner, propped up with pillows, lay the aged woman whose strong features in which the remembrance to her Indian ancestors was plainly visible, were convulsed in their last agony. The gray hair was thrown back from the dark old face, and the tall frame seemed almost that of a giantress. One hand lay outside the coverlet, the other reposed on her heart. Just before the end came she roused herself and tried to speak. The dusky figures gathered around her and strained their ears to listen for her words, but it was in vain. The noble pioneer negress had finished a career of exceptional usefulness and was dead.

The *Central City Register-Call* editorialized on Clara's passing in its October 30, 1885, issue:

> To the pioneers of Central City, "Aunt Clara" needs no eulogy. The name, "Aunt Clara Brown" calls to mind the dignified, gentle nature of her who bore it.

She was deeply religious, and often a miner returning to his shack has seen Aunt Clara alone on the mountainside, praying for the miners underground. Her character and her good deeds made her one of Central City's most respected and beloved citizens. Clara's death came less than two years after being reunited with her daughter. The funeral service on October 27 was held at Denver's Central Presbyterian Church and arranged by the Society of Colorado Pioneers, which had made Clara its first honorary Black member. Reverend E. P. Wells officiated. The Zion Baptist Choir provided the music. Among those in attendance were the governor and the city mayor. The *Denver Tribune-Republican* captured in print moments from the funeral service in its October 29, 1885, issue:

> The Reverend E. P. Wells gave an animated sketch of "Aunt" Clara's life, mingled with personal reminiscences, he having been acquainted with her for a period of seventeen years. He recounted her many struggles in Colorado,

> her life of labor and self-denial, and the large amount of money she had saved and expanded in bringing to Colorado other freed blacks.

Clara's body was laid to rest in Denver's Riverside Cemetery. However, in 1896, Harriet Mason, a member of one of the many families Clara had helped move west, had Clara's remains reburied in her family plot. Thus there are two markers to Clara Brown in the cemetery.

Today Clara is remembered in Colorado history as courageous, kind, devoted, and deserving of great respect. Her legacy is commemorated by a stained-glass window in the Colorado State Capitol, a bronze plaque at the St. James Methodist Church in Central City, and an honorary chair in the Central City Opera House. In 2015, a bronze statue of her likeness was erected in the new African American Museum of the Smithsonian Institute in Washington D.C.

As stated in her induction to the Society of Colorado Pioneers:

> Clara Brown was a kind old friend whose heart always responded to the cry of distress, and who, rising from the humble position of slave to the angelic type of a noble woman, won out sympathy and commanded our respect.

GOLDEN

The Elusive "Mountain Charley"

> *Friend G---:*
>
> *I cannot wait to thank you for your unselfish kindness to me, and that of your pards. I must be in Gregory Gulch by 10 o'clock to-day or perhaps lose the opportunity of my strange life in the mountains. I cannot wait to catch my mule but will walk to Tucker's Gulch and get a pony from John Soot for the trip. Will you please have her stabled for me by Saturday, when I will be down, and can then, perhaps, fulfill my promise to you of giving you something of my history. Be sure you are the only man, woman or child west of the Missouri river that will ever have it from my lips. I am dreadfully tired, but I must go to Gregory this morning.*
>
> *Good bye till Saturday.*
>
> *Charley* [16]

This note to George West of Golden was one of many Mountain Charley would send to her friend and closest confidant. For George West was one of a very few who knew the true identity of the woman who called herself "Mountain Charley."

She first sought out her fortune in gold in the California Gold Rush of 1849, having made her way there by 1851. She met with some success but upon hearing of the great Pikes Peak Gold Rush in 1858, Mountain Charley set out for the Colorado Rocky Mountains.

Many tales abound around the elusive Mountain Charley, many of which can be attributed to the woman herself. In any case, this is the story of Mountain Charley and her experiences in the Colorado goldfields.

She was born Elsa Jane Forest in Baton Rouge, Louisiana, in approximately 1837.[17] According to her own autobiography, *An Autobiography Comprising a Period of Thirteen Years in the States, California and Pikes Peak*, which was published in 1861, Elsa was married with two young children by the time she was fifteen. It was at this point in her life that events set her on a far different path than she could have ever imagined.

Elsa's husband, who is never referred to by name, was a Mississippi riverboat pilot. Early one morning he was shot and murdered on the boat by a man named Jamieson. Now widowed, alone with two toddlers, Elsa Jane needed to find a way to support her family. Yet she knew the difficulties women faced, for she later wrote, "I knew how great are the prejudices to be overcome by any young woman who seeks to earn an honest livelihood by her own exertions."[18]

Elsa soon learned she was nothing if not shrewd, conniving, and most of all, convincing. She claimed financial hardship and was able to persuade the Sisters of Charity to take in her two children. Next, she cut her hair, donned men's attire, and changed the tone of her voice. As she wrote, "I buried my sex in my heart and roughened the surface so that the grave would not be discovered—as men of the plains cache some treasure and build a fire over the spot so that the charred embers may hide the secret."[19]

With her new identity, Elsa needed a new name. She called herself "Charley." She found work in various capacities, as a cabin boy on a steamship and as a freighter, and even worked for the railroad. In time she began to enjoy her new life and the opportunities it afforded.

> I began to rather like the freedom of my new character. I could go where I chose, do many things which while innocent in themselves, were debarred

> by propriety from association with the female sex. The change from the cumbersome, unhealthy attire of women to the more convenient healthy habilaments of a man, was in itself almost sufficient to compensate for its unwomanly character.

Charley worked on various riverboats for nearly four years before obtaining railroad work in St. Louis in 1854. Once a month she changed into a dress and visited her children. While in St. Louis, Charley happened to learn that Jamieson, the man who had murdered her husband, was staying at a nearby hotel. After spending considerable time tracking him down, Charley finally confronted him on a chilly night outside the Schell Saloon. After introducing herself, Charley pulled her pistol and squeezed the trigger. Her shot missed. Jamieson drew his revolver and fired twice. The second shot hit Charley in the leg. Jamieson ran off and Charley managed to make her way to the back alley where she fainted.

A widow by the name of Mrs. Anderson found her and took her into her home, and there Charley stayed nearly six months until her wound had healed. During this time she read newspaper accounts of the California Gold Rush and made plans to join the gold seekers and make her fortune. In the spring of 1855, she joined a wagon train headed west. Charley kept a journal of this trip that offers great insights to the westward travels of those early pioneers. Her descriptions of the hard work, weather conditions, and especially the rugged landmarks along the trail, such as Courthouse and Chimney Rocks, and Independence Rock, are spellbinding.

Unfortunately, California was a bust for Charley. But she loved the adventure. In the spring of 1859, she was ready to try her luck again when she learned of the new gold rush in the Rocky Mountains. Her first foray was panning for gold at the base of Pikes Peak. But like many other gold seekers would learn, there was no gold and "Pikes Peak or Bust" was just an advertising slogan. As she later noted:

> I stayed in this country till the Pike's [*sic*] Peak fever broke out, when I came back to the States, and spent a few weeks with my children. I then started for Pike's Peak, going by the Santa Fe Mail route in the spring of 1859. At that time it was but an incipient place, there being but one log cabin in the place.
>
> I immediately went to prospecting for gold, and continued at that for about three months and met with no success. About this time gold was discovered by [John] Gregory in the mountains [Gregory Gulch], and following in the wake of the excitement which the event produced, I went thither and

> located myself about forty-two miles from Denver City [in Central City]. I met with good success, and was making money rapidly, when in the Fall I was taken sick with the mountain fever, and giving up went back to Denver.

When Charley's gold prospects washed out, she returned to Denver City where she bought a saloon on Blake Street with what little money she had made. She named it the "Mountain Boy's Saloon." It became a popular local hangout, despite its occasional bar fights. The following news clip appeared in the September 10, 1859, issue of *The Rocky Mountain News:*

> Locals, of stirring interest, are scarce this week. There have been two or three fights at the Mountain Boys Saloon, but our local, who has a wholesome respect for his corporal safety in this land of bowie knives and pistols, seldom gets near enough the scene of a row to learn the particulars.

Charley's customers soon dubbed her "Mountain Charley" and the moniker stuck. She later wrote, "My right name is Charlotte so you see I have a right to the one I adopted, masculine though it might be." In October, *The Rocky Mountain News* featured Charley, describing her as "the veritable and notorious Charley, smoking, drinking, swearing, and consorting with men."

In the early summer of 1859, Mountain Charley was returning to Denver from a brief trip to Golden when she crossed paths with none other than her nemesis, Jamieson. In true wild west fashion, still on horseback, each drew their guns. Jamieson missed, Charley did not. "I emptied my revolver upon him as he lay," she wrote, "and should have done the same with its mate had not two hunters at the moment came upon the ground and prevented any further consummation of my designs."

Nevertheless, the hunters aided Charley in her predicament by building a litter and hauling the wounded man to Denver. Jamieson recovered from his wounds and told everyone within earshot that Mountain Charley wasn't to blame; that he did, in fact, kill her husband. Then Jamieson quickly left town. With this revelation, Charley's true gender was revealed. She became a bit of a celebrity in Denver City and her old stomping grounds of Golden. With her true identity known, Charley was now free to marry her bartender, H. L. Guerin. "I continued in my male attire notwithstanding the knowledge of my sex," she wrote, "and kept my saloon during the winter of 1859-60. I had a bar-keeper, named H. L. Guerin, whom I married, and in the spring we sold out the saloon and went into the mountains where we opened a boarding house and commenced mining."

After another winter season prospecting in the Rocky Mountains, Charley and her husband decided to return to St. Louis and her children. But before she did, she made arrangements to meet with her old friend, General George West, who would become the publisher and editor of Golden's newspaper, the *Colorado Transcript.*

> My good friend G—
> My 'prospecting' is done in these mountains! I am concealed here at Guy Gulch because I do not want to go to Golden, and I have one more favor to ask of you, and it will probably be the last one, for I am going away. I want you to come to me in the morning, before sun-up, with my mule. Cinch her up good and tight when you put the saddle on, for I don't want to risk it turning on me. I'll be at the hogback north of Dick Bright's ranch waiting for you. If you can spare the time come with one of your horses and ride with me long enough for me to keep my promise to you. I must tell my story to some one, for it is burning my heart out. You have been my friend and must hear it, or it shall die with me. You'll be at the hogback in the morning I am sure. I shall be waiting for there by daylight. I am glad I came to the mountains. I am glad I am going away from the mountains. The altitude is too great. Good bye till morning.

West was eager to keep this appointment for he had wanted to get Mountain Charley's story down on paper for quite some time. He later wrote, "From frequent meetings upon the road, and long rides together both in the valleys and mountains, I had become interested in her strange conduct, and on several occasions had attempted an 'interview' but totally without success until circumstances threw her under my protection."

George West and Mountain Charley met several times, and West devoted himself to telling her story. But Charley had a stipulation; West was not to publish her account for twenty-five years. West wrote at the time, "This was the last I have ever seen or heard of 'Mountain Charley.'"

West finally published Mountain Charley's story in a series for his newspaper, the *Colorado Transcript,* beginning with the January 14, 1885, issue. In a remarkable set of circumstances Charley saw the issue and wrote to West from her home in Dubuque, Iowa.

> My old friend G. W.:
> You may well realize my surprise when yesterday I was shown a copy of your paper by a friend who is in residence of a neighboring town, and whose husband had been a subscriber for a number of years. This lady was much interested in

> your sketch of Mountain Charley, as she said her husband well remembered her when he was a resident of Golden twenty-five years ago, and had often wondered what had become of the strange girl so well known in the Rocky Mountains.
>
> My surprise and interest were also great as was my gratification to find that you had kept your promise made to me so many years ago. And now, in part payment for the kindly manner in which you have treated my wild escapade, fully assured that my secret, so far as it relates to my present whereabouts will be safe with you, I resolved to at once write to you of it.
>
> You befriended me when I was in a great straight, and I feel that it is only justice that you should have the story of my life after we were separated. I send you with this a little memorandum book which contains the diary kept by me of all the important incidents in my strange life. Use it as you think best. If you use my diary to complete the story of my wild, strange masquerade as 'Mountain Charley' it may prove of interest to many of the old timers - 'Barnacles' I see you call them now, and I shall be satisfied as long as they have no means of penetrating our secret.
>
> Good by and God bless you.

West ended his series about the infamous Mountain Charley with this final thought:

> Upon her earnest solicitation nothing more will be given of the life of this strange character after her return to her life. The reader already knows, from the letter published at the commencement of this sequel, that she is happily married and with a tenderly loving husband and a family of loving children around her, is passing her declining years in a sphere suited to her sex, loved and respected by all who know her.

And with that, no more was ever revealed about the elusive Mountain Charley.

GILPIN COUNTY

Angeline Louisiana Munn: "Gold Woman" of Gilpin County

> Munn, Angeline Louisiana: Miner
> b. Henry, La. Sept. 6, 1890. ed. Henry, La pub sch: St. Normal Sch, La. Teachers Cert.

m. Arthur Neil Munn (dec) Dec. 16, 1932 in Golden, Colo. int var mining in diff parts of Colorado, int in Russell Gulch, Gregory Gulch, Alma Co. sev properties the primary ones Washington mine. Gold Woman of Colo Elks Parade. public benefactor. res. Bankers row, Central City.

As this entry in the 1938 *Who's Who of Colorado* indicates, Angeline Louisiana Munn was not only a celebrity in Colorado's social scene, but an accomplished businesswoman as well. And it all came from gold mines in the "Richest Square Mile on Earth."

She was born Angeline Louisiana Huff on September 6, 1890, in Vermillion Parish, Louisiana. Angie Lou, as she was called, was the seventh of ten children born to Edward and Angela Huff. The Huffs were wealthy rice farmers in the Louisiana bayou country. Following high school graduation, Angie Lou attended the Louisiana Normal College (now Northwestern State University), beginning in 1910. She earned a teaching certificate and taught school for five years.

Angeline Munn promoted herself as the "Gold Woman of Colorado." PHOTOGRAPH COURTESY OF THE AUTHOR.

At some point she made her way to Colorado and married Arthur Neil Munn on December 16, 1923. Munn, twenty-four years old, hailed from Ozark, Alabama, and was a district salesman for the Goldman Shoe Company.

A few years after her marriage, Angie began investing in Colorado mines. It is not known where or how she acquired her investment money. It surely was not from her husband's shoe salesman salary, but possibly from an inheritance after her father's passing in 1913. By the 1930s many of Colorado's mines had either played out or were too expensive to operate as the country's economy sank into the Great Depression.

In any case, Angie's investments in Cripple Creek mines proved fairly successful. Angie was smitten with gold fever. She employed the services of a highly respected prospector, Hugh Higham, who scouted for gold mines on her behalf.[20] Higham located a few promising properties in McCullough Gulch, not far from Breckenridge in Summit County.

Angie Munn was determined to be present in a hands-on manner and be involved in the development of the mines. In 1932, forty-two-year-old Angie first trekked into the mountains to view her new properties, a total of seven, including the Noon Day Sun Mine. Perched at 10,000 feet above sea level, Angie was the first white woman ever to reach this particular mountaintop. For the next three years Angie worked on her mines, developing them into highly profitable gold mines. It was quite gratifying as well as a learning experience for Angie—experience she intended to put to good use.

In the summer of 1936, Angie was introduced to an old Gilpin County prospector named Wilson. He informed her of the rich gold deposits still left in and around Central City and Black Hawk. Wilson believed, despite the economic depression that gripped the entire country, that many of the mines in the "Richest Square Mile on Earth," as Gilpin County had become famous for, could again be profitable in time. Intrigued by the prospects, Angie and her trusted mining engineer, Hugh Higham, traveled to Central City to have a look at Wilson's mining claims.

On May 7, 1937, Angie engaged the services of John H. Marks, a noted hydraulic and civil engineer based in Denver. By May 18, 1937, Marks had completed his survey of the Gilpin County mines that Angie was interested in and provided her with his report. He charged her $123.47 for this service.[21]

Of the many mines, the Washington was the most promising, as it branched off a vein of the fabulously wealthy Bobtail Mine within the town limits of Central City. The physical description and location of the mine was included in Marks' report, a portion of which reads:

> This lode mining property is in the Gregory Mining District, Gilpin County, Colorado. It is in or near the corporate limits of the towns of Central City and Blackhawk, altitude approximates 8500 feet above sea level. Central City is the county seat of Gilpin County and is less than two hours by automobile

> from Denver. A branch line of the Colorado and Southern railway runs to Blackhawk, which town is about one mile from the Munn Washington tunnel.
>
> The Washington mine, U.S. Mineral Survey No. 611 contains an area of 4.6 acres, patented and is in the vicinity of many of the old time pay mines of the Central City district. Of the title to this property, I am informed you have data, and also that Mrs. A. L. Munn has abstract of title.[22]

Originally located and developed in 1880, the Washington Mine was one of many rich ore producers in the gold "Kingdom of Gilpin." Perfectly situated between two rich gold veins, one being the famous Bobtail lode, the mine had several shafts and tunnels on various levels. The discovery shaft alone was documented to be 205 feet deep. Marks knew there was rich paying ore deep in the mine, but how much ore? And how rich? In his report, Marks noted his reasoning and listed the sample findings. He also cited another engineer's report on the mine:

> A one page report describing equipment and present condition of the mine is included herewith, prepared by Mr. John L. Robson, M.E., consulting engineer on the Washington mine. Mr. Robson is an experienced mining engineer, a graduate of Colorado School of Mines, has a "nose" for ore, and is, I think, the right man in the right place. This report also points out assay samplings that were taken.[23]

The nine assay samples ranged from "grab samples," randomly taken from the soil, to veins as thin as two inches to as thick as two feet. Values were from $4.90 per ton to as much as $42 per ton. While this was nowhere near the values of the initial 1859 gold rush, given the economic depression of the 1930s, the value was still promising. What really sealed the deal for Marks and Angie Munn was a possible tie into the Bobtail lode that the survey also revealed:

> Patent notes also describe some 30 holes, cuts and shafts, varying in depth from 3 to 30 feet. In addition there is described a deep shaft 'depth unknown' on east end of Washington lode. These numerous workings suggest that the object of these investigations may have been an effort to determine if surface values might exist, similar to the famous 'Patch' at Nevadaville. It might be that surface exploration of the Washington mine would disclose ore that could be mined from surface by steam shovel or 'glory hole' methods.

> It appears that Washington vein has not yet been located on the east end of the slain, and that drift run northwesterly from the end of the Bobtail tunnel level on south side of Washington would cut it. The Bobtail lode should extend into the east end of the Washington lode.

Angie's mining experts proposed a bold plan to make the Washington Mine profitable. Development began on the east side of the claim where the vein ran directly to the Bobtail tunnel. The plan worked and within a year the Washington Mine was producing over $75,000 in gold.

With her newfound wealth, Angie purchased a fine home on Central City's Banker's Row area. This home still stands at 205 East 1st High Street. It is interesting to note that the deed to the property was in Angie's name alone.

Although Angie had been living separately from her husband, the two never divorced. Sadly, within a year of Angie's mining successes, Arthur Munn died. Angie quickly discovered that Munn's employer had been withholding commissions as well as other financial promises. Angie sued. In the end a settlement was reached and Angie received just under $300,000.[24]

Angeline Munn on the grounds of the Washington Mine. PHOTOGRAPH COURTESY OF THE AUTHOR.

At the same time, Angie's star was rising on the social scene. Her success as a businesswoman, because of or despite her gender, endeared her to the elite societies of both Central City and Denver. Along with her entry in *Who's Who of Colorado,* Angie's name was constantly in the society columns of local newspapers. Even the

New York Times took notice of Angie Munn. In the August 1, 1937, issue, under the headline, "Gold in Them Thar Hills," Angie's mining success was told in all its glory. Angie even took the reporter through one of the tunnels of her Washington Mine and gave him a gold nugget worth $10.[25]

After being featured in the country's top newspaper, Angie had bigger ambitions. She bought Denver's prestigious hostelry, the Windsor Hotel. Once the pride of Denver, it had quickly fallen out of favor after construction of the Brown Palace Hotel and then completion of silver baron Horace A. W. Tabor's grand opus, the Tabor Block.

The Windsor was built on nine lots at the corner of Eighteenth and Larimer Streets. An English investor, James Duff, of the Colorado Mortgage and Investment Company, commissioned $500,000 to build the lavish hotel, which was five stories high and 225 feet long. Before the Windsor was completed, however, Tabor leased the entire hotel. He spent nearly $200,000 furnishing it, and continued to have a controlling interest until he lost everything in the Silver Panic of 1893. From then on, the once opulent establishment fell out of favor with the general public. By the time Angie Munn took an interest, in 1938, the Windsor was a place for vagrants. Some of these people committed suicide by jumping over the stair rails onto the marble floor below. Because it was such a regular occurrence, the back stairway became known as the "Suicide Stairway."

Now in dire condition, not to mention its grim reputation, Angie picked up the hotel property for a song from Robert W. Speer, a former mayor of Denver. She set out to restore it to its former glory. However, shortly after the purchase, Speer loaded up four moving vans full of the hotel's original furnishings. Fortunately enough for Angie, many of the Tabor furnishings remained from the period, nearly fifty years earlier, when Horace and his beloved Baby Doe lived at the Windsor.

Over the next ten years, Angie made a variety of improvements to the hotel. She refurbished the ballroom and opened a nightclub in 1940. Angie invited famed artist Herndon Davis to paint murals of famous Windsor guests. The nightclub was the most popular hangout in all of Denver all through the war years.

Angie enjoyed hosting parties and elaborate dances at her hotel, particularly because she loved being the belle of the ball. Denver's elite society, as well as politicians, never missed an invitation to be seen at Windsor Hotel. Governor Ralph Carr and Denver Mayor Benjamin Stapleton were among Angie's closet friends.

Apparently Angie enjoyed the hotel business so much so that in 1946, she and her sister, Lillian Campbell Hargraves, bought the historic Creede Hotel. The small hotel in the San Juan mountain mining town was purchased for the unbelievably small sum of $5,000. This storied hotel had also lost its original glamour and lore, so the sisters set about restoring it to its former glory.

Angie also bought a house in Creede and dabbled in mining. Although there are a few mining records with her involvement, she never met with the success she did in Central City. Nevertheless, Creede became her permanent home. She continued with her love of parties and social gatherings, although on a much smaller scale.

In 1968, due to Lillian's failing health, Angie sold the Creede Hotel. A few years later, Lillian died and was buried in the Creede cemetery.

Two years later, on February 2, 1970. Angeline Louisiana Munn died. She was eighty years old. She was buried in the Creede cemetery next to her sister.

Her estate left something of a mystery behind. There was no money. But there were deeds to her mining claims in both Summit and Gilpin Counties.

Perhaps this was a clue to what the mining lady truly valued. ✦

Notes

1. Auraria would later merge with its rival camp across the river, Denver City.
2. Marshall, Thomas M. *Early Records of Gilpin County 1859-1861.* University of Colorado, 1920. p. 7.
3. Noel, Thomas J. *Denver, Rocky Mountain Gold,* 1980. p. 22.
4. Bonnie, Sue. Four-part series titled "Baby Doe Tabor." *True Story Magazine*, 1937. This was actually commissioned and written by Caroline Bancroft using Bonnie's notes from her many conversations with Baby Doe.
5. Bancroft, Caroline. *Gulch of Gold: A History of Central City, Colorado.* Johnson Books, 2003. p. 282.
6. Gilpin County Archives, Central City, Colorado.
7. Over the years Baby Doe made several scrapbooks. The majority are in the Tabor collection at Colorado History Center. Two are in the possession of Colorado author and former president of the Gilpin County Historical Society, Linda Jones' and her heirs.
8. Some writers have maintained that the baby was actually Sandelowsky's. This author cannot substantiate that claim.
9. Scrapbook in the possession of Linda Jones' heirs.
10. Parkhill, Forbes. *Wildest of the West.* Henry Holt and Co., 1951. p. 155.
11. This is the same judge who would later preside over the divorce of Horace and Augusta Tabor.

12. Beardsley, Isaac Haight. *Echoes From Peak and Plain: Or Tales of Life, War, Travel and Colorado Methodism.* Kessinger Publishing, 2010. p. 358.
13. The name of Clara's husband is unknown. Various writers have assumed his name was Richard as that was the name of their only son.
14. Information provided by Roger Baker. Gilpin County Record book number 38, p. 579.
15. Mr. Thatcher was Joseph Thatcher, president of the First National Bank of Central City.
16. All letters from Elsa aka "Mountain Charley" as well as the quotes of General George West, are from his series titled "Mountain Charley: A Sequel." Published in the January and February 1885 issues of his paper, the *Colorado Transcript.*
17. In her autobiography she gives her age in several recounted incidents and from this her birth date is deduced.
18. This book was reprinted in 1968 by the sensational Fred Mazzulla with the equally sensational title, *Mountain Charley or the Adventures of Mrs. E. J. Guerin, who was thirteen years in male attire.* University of Oklahoma Press, 1965. All quotes of Mountain Charley are from this work.
19. ibid.
20. Hargraves, Orin. "The Fabulous Life of Angeline Louisiana Munn." https://okh.medium.com/the-fabulous-life-of-angeline-louisiana-munn-afbfd98bf914. 2019. p. 7.
21. 1938 Washington Mine Survey, Gilpin County, Colorado. Gilpin County Archives.
22. ibid.
23. ibid.
24. Hargraves. "The Fabulous Life of Angeline Louisiana Munn." p. 15.
25. Dallas, Sandra. *No More Than Five in a Bed: Colorado Hotels in the Old Days.* University of Oklahoma Press, 1967. p. 103.

2

THE SILVER QUEEN

IDAHO SPRINGS

THOUSANDS OF GOLD SEEKERS flocked to the Colorado Rocky Mountains during the Pikes Peak or Bust Gold Rush of 1858–1859. While most were concentrated over the pass at Central City and Black Hawk, George Jackson followed Chicago Creek upstream. He found large quantities of gold in the stream and staked a few claims in January 1859.

A mining camp was formed, first named Idahoe, and it was platted on June 22, 1860. Following territorial status, Clear Creek County became one of the original seventeen counties formed, with Idahoe as the county seat, designated on November 15, 1861. On April 7, 1876, the year of Colorado statehood, the town name was officially changed to Idaho Springs.

Placer mining thrived until about 1865. Both gold and silver were mined until it became obvious that the veins revealing the richest ores were deep in the rocky mountainsides. Though few got rich, many were able to make a living and provide for their families.

When the price of silver plummeted due to the government no longer backing silver and the repeal of the Sherman Silver Purchase Act, Idaho Springs was in a unique spot—literally and figuratively. From 1893 and through both world wars, gold production dominated.

To help facilitate this ore production, the Newhouse Tunnel was built in 1893. A drainage and transportation tunnel, it was driven toward Central City, some four and a half miles. It would take ten years to build and was completed in 1903. The operation added a mill, constructed in 1913. The tunnel made it easier to bring the gold to the surface while also allowing for better drainage and ventilation. The Colorado and Southern narrow gauge railroad ran directly to the tunnel entrance, providing swift ore transportation. Eventually, the name was changed to the Argo Tunnel and Mill, both of which were state of the art and provided additional services to Idaho Springs and points beyond, such as mine connection through the tunnel operation and milling services for the mines in and around Clear Creek County.

Ida Stingley Newhouse: Glamour and Mystery

Ida Stingley Newhouse used her beauty and her keen sense of business acumen to attract investors for her husband's mining ventures. She would carry out her husband's business affairs with uncanny precision and leave an air of mystery about her.

Ida Stingley was born in Virginia in 1863, at the height of the Civil War. When her father died later that year, Ida's mother, Mary, found herself alone to raise her young children. Over the next few years, Mary took her children on the westward journey risked by so many others.

Eventually Mary settled in Leadville where she ran a boarding house for miners at 118 West Sixth Street.[1] When Ida was old enough, she helped her mother serve meals to the boarders. One of those men was Samuel Newhouse. The two were soon smitten with one another although Ida was only fifteen years old. Ida begged her mother to not charge the young man for his meals.[2] Apparently Ida had no idea Newhouse came from a wealthy family.

As she came of age, Ida was among the debutante girls of the season. The society column of the *Leadville Daily Herald* commented on the beauty and attire of Miss Ida Stingley. Gossip tongues wagged, and even the *Leadville Daily Herald* of December 16, 1882, devoted space to the pairing of Ida and twenty-nine-year-old Samuel Newhouse at a Christmas party.

Samuel Newhouse was born October 14, 1853, to Russian Jewish immigrant parents in New York City. He attended school in Pennsylvania and intended to pursue a career in law when he was sidelined by a keen interest in mining. Newhouse left the East Coast bound for the West and mining riches.

Arriving in Leadville, Newhouse worked in several different mines, finally deciding underground mining was not for him. It during this time that he met Ida Stingley. Newhouse later said, "I was a miner with nothing but my dreams. I worked like a miner. I'll never forget Ida Stingley as she looked to me that first time I saw her and decided to see her again. Our first home was in Leadville. It was small, yes, and built of logs."[3]

The couple were wed in Leadville on January 1, 1883, at the home of Ida's sister. Following a traveling honeymoon by train, the couple returned to Leadville where Newhouse bought a hotel and began investing in mining properties.

One of those properties was the Newhouse Tunnel in Idaho Springs. In 1893, Newhouse took over the entire operation and spearheaded the completion of the tunnel to Central City. He named the tunnel after himself.

In those early years, to keep his property operating, Newhouse enlisted his wife to secure financial backing. A flamboyant promoter himself, Newhouse knew Ida's beauty and social appeal would win over even the shrewdest of investors. Newhouse hired a tutor to educate his wife in the manner of high society. He then sent Ida to the East Coast to meet with his business contacts. His idea worked. Ida used her newly developed personal skills and her beauty to attract investors.

Ida seemed to enjoy her new role and the power she gained. Soon, she was off to Europe and was able to secure finances for the next Newhouse enterprise, the Argo Mill in Idaho Springs. This new mill, when completed, would bring more jobs to Idaho Springs and allow for gold to be processed on-site, rather than shipped over high passes to other mills. The mill would actually extend the gold production in the area by making it more profitable.

The Newhouse Tunnel and Argo Mill helped mines in Idaho Springs remain profitable and made Ida and Samuel Newhouse wealthy. PHOTOGRAPH COURTESY OF DENVER PUBLIC LIBRARY, SPECIAL COLLECTIONS.

Was financial backing a continual problem or did Ida simply enjoy the task? Either way, she was constantly traveling to the East Coast and abroad where she became great friends with England's Prince of Wales, the future King Edward VII.

Due to his wife's great skills in securing financial backing, Newhouse was able to expand his mining properties to silver and copper in the majestic canyons of Utah. Meanwhile, Ida continued her work abroad and secured the needed finances for investing in mining properties in Cripple Creek. The *Cripple Creek Times* issue dated December 17, 1895, reported:

> A letter received from Mr. Newhouse said he had interested several Londoners in Colorado mines, principally those of Cripple Creek and at a dinner given by Baron Rotheschilde [*sic*] a company had been organized for investing over here. The next day the full capitalization, $2,500,000 was paid in and Mr. Newhouse was instructed to use his own judgment in placing it.

As it turned out, the Newhouses did not invest in Cripple Creek mines, but rather in Ouray mines. All the while Newhouse poured money into his Argo Tunnel and Mill.

By the turn of the century, the mines were beginning to play out and so was the Newhouse money. There was also the matter of the Newhouse lifestyle. The society column of the *Leadville Herald Democrat* dated February 3, 1902, reported:

> And pearls! Well, you ought to see that one string her husband gave her! It cost $150,000—just a string to go once around her throat, mind you.

Life was a lavish party put on by the Newhouse couple.

When World War I broke out it was nearly impossible to travel to Europe, let alone obtain any sort of financial capital in a time of war. However, Ida managed to get to England where she turned her attention to the war effort. In a letter to her husband, Ida wrote, "I must go to England and care for the boys who are suffering. I have determined that I can do better work there in the hospitals than I can here."[4]

A year later, Ida and Samuel Newhouse separated. Ida preferred to remain in England. Ida lived a long storied life, one of intrigue and a bit of mystery. Through it all, she had an extreme impact on the mining economy of Idaho Springs.

Ida Stingley Newhouse died of pneumonia in a nursing home in 1955 at the age of ninety-one.

Today, the Argo Mill and Tunnel are open for tours. They remain a masterpiece in mining ingenuity courtesy of Ida Newhouse and her ways with money.

Silver Queen of the Rockies: GEORGETOWN

When George Jackson discovered gold on Chicago Creek in 1859, a mad dash of prospectors covered the mountain valleys like so many ants to a picnic. Late to the prospecting party were brothers George and David Griffith. Seeing that most of the good claims were taken, the brothers moved upstream. Panning for gold yielded very little for the Griffith brothers, so they continued up the mountain valley.

Then in August 1859, the brothers saw a promising spot and within a few days they had panned approximately $500 in gold. They followed the clear stream to the side of a mountain. There they discovered a rich vein but kept quiet. It was essentially a silver-bearing lode with surface quartz of gold. A few years would pass before it was determined that the discovery did indeed contain silver—and a lot of it.

In the meantime, they brought up a sluice box and continued to wash the precious gold metal out of the creek bed, later known as South Clear Creek. This was near the corner of Eleventh and Rose Streets in present-day Georgetown. The brothers staked their claim and the following year established the Griffith Mining District. George became District Recorder and named the new mining camp "George's Town."

The little mining camp nearly exploded in population overnight when on September 14, 1864, high-grade silver was discovered on McClellen Mountain south of the mining hamlet. It assayed at $800 to the ton. It was the richest silver strike in the state to date. The Argentine Mining District was established to handle all the silver claims. However, it wasn't until 1868 that a smelting process for silver was perfected that allowed for ease of production and increase of profits.

When the Territorial Legislature granted a town charter in 1868, George's Town became Georgetown and was known as the Silver Queen of the Rockies for decades.

Margaret Coburn Hoskins: A Miner's Wife Filled with Tragedy

Life in any mountain mining camp was hard. It came with hard lessons. It was hard living. It was heartache. Walking through any cemetery near a mining town is a testament to that hard life.

One of the first cemeteries I visited as a child with my parents was the Alvarado Cemetery just outside of Georgetown. The children's graves were what stayed with me at that young time in my life. Years later, while researching for my book, *From the Grave: Colorado's Pioneer Cemeteries,* I went back to that haunting cemetery. Such a sad, forlorn resting place it is. Full of young people gone too soon. The story of Margaret Coburn Hoskins can be found in this cemetery. Hers is just one of many sad tales of that hard life.

Margaret Coburn was just fourteen years old when she and her parents, John and Margaret, journeyed west for a better life. The family arrived in Georgetown in 1871. It must have been exciting to live in such a bustling mountain mining camp as Georgetown. John Coburn built a fine home for his family and started a hotel.

Maggie, as she was known, enjoyed school and making friends over the next few years. She went to socials, dances, teas, and the like. But it was at a local baseball game in 1873 that a chance meeting changed her life forever. The Georgetown Nine were playing the Central City Stars. A young Cornish miner, twenty-two-year-old James Hoskins played outfield for the home team. Sixteen-year-old Maggie was smitten.

Three years later, James and Maggie were married at Georgetown's Methodist Episcopal Church, on February 29, 1876.[5] James worked in several mines and the couple moved often. From Lawson to Clear Creek and from Freeland to Georgetown, Maggie always made her home a happy one.

That happiness was shattered by tragedy when William, Maggie's firstborn child, died at birth on April 9, 1877.[6] The couple had more children, and by 1884, James and Maggie were living back in Georgetown where James was a partner, along with Gerald Bressette and Aldrich Delphy, in the Virginia City Mining Company.

Death dealt Maggie another blow when on December 23, 1888, her beloved father, John Coburn, died. The two were extremely close and his death hit Maggie hard.

Less than a month later, Maggie's world began to unravel. On January 10, 1889, the Hoskinses' woodshed burned to the ground. On February 15, 1889, Hoskins' mining partner, Gerald Bressette, disappeared. A posse tracked footprints in the snow to the base of Empire Pass where the trail was lost. Law enforcement began to believe Bressette was involved in some sort of mining fraud and had left town one step ahead of the law. As the gossip spread like the wind, Hoskins began to take precautions. He kept his horse saddled in the barn every night, as he felt his life was in danger. Why? What did he really know about his partner's disappearance?

A month later, on March 27, 1889, Maggie found James Hoskins with a gunshot wound to the head. Maggie did what she could to keep him alive, and the next day two local doctors performed surgery. It was too late; there was little they could do. On March 29, 1889, James Hoskins died.

Maggie remembered his unusual behavior early on the morning of the 27th. He was angry, agitated, and pacing the floor with a Colt revolver in his hand. Again the gossip whispered about town. Was it suicide, or was it murder? During the autopsy, the recovered bullet did not match the Colt revolver.[7] Murder. But who? And why? Gerald Bressette had disappeared, never to be found. The murder's mystery was never solved.

James' death left Maggie rattled and nearly destitute. She took in boarders, sold book subscriptions, and did other odd jobs to support herself and her children. Then tragedy struck again. On August 25, 1890, Maggie's youngest child, Florence, called Tot, died at eight years old.

The death of her youngest child seemed to be the final blow for Maggie's once happy life. She withdrew from life day by day until she finally died on August 27, 1895. Margaret "Maggie" Coburn Hoskins was thirty-eight years young.

A silent stroll through the Alvarado Cemetery will reveal the Hoskins family plot. There is a marker for James, but nothing to mark the burial spot of Maggie or her beloved children.

SILVER PLUME

Farther upstream on Clear Creek from Georgetown, the mining camp of Silver Plume was established on September 15, 1870, and incorporated ten years later. There are two versions as to how the name came about. One is that the town was named after a nearby silver mine. The other is that the name was inspired by a vein of silver so rich that silver seemed to flake off in tiny feather-like pieces.

The earliest known silver strike was in 1860, but like the discoveries closer to Georgetown and the Griffith brothers' claim, nobody then knew how rich the deposits were. In any case, by 1870, they knew what they had—silver. By 1879 the population was 1,500 and topped 2,000 by 1890.

I miss the snowy hills of home
They keep becoming to me
I'm going back to Silver Plume
That is where I want to be
And Silver Plume is just the place

Try it out and you will know
It's just next door to Heaven
In sunshine or in snow

Longtime Silver Plume resident Mary Ellen Barnes wrote this ode to her beloved hometown and titled it "The White Gold."

And so it was. Silver Plume was a miner's town, while Georgetown was a mine owner's town. Silver Plume lay at the base of the mountain where the rich Argentine silver mine had been located. The spectacular Pelican and Dives Mines were also here, and the Terrible Mine, owned by Georgetown millionaire William Hamill. The monument to the Seven-Thirty Mine owner, Clifford Griffin, is high on the mountaintop above town. Legend and lore lies around Silver Plume and hovers above as well.

Silver by the ore load was dug from these mountains. Soon the mining tents gave way to neat little wooden houses along neat little dirt streets. Families required schools and churches. On Main Street, businesses flourished. There were supply stores, mercantiles, dry goods, a newspaper office, a candy store, and even an opera house. In November 1884, a disastrous fire swept through the entire town. Businesses and many homes burned to the ground. The community pulled together and quickly rebuilt.

Alice Griffin "Ma" Buckley: The Heart of the Community

One member of the dedicated community that was Silver Plume was Alice Griffin Buckley. Alice's parents, Ellen Short and Daniel Griffin, came west, like so many others, following the Civil War. They settled in Nevadaville, above Central City, where their first child, Alice, was born on November 8, 1862. It is said Alice Griffin was the first white child born in Gilpin County. Daniel Griffin found work in the mines near Nevadaville and Central City.

Alice was but a toddler when her father was killed in a duel in Central City. Left to fend for herself and her child, Ellen Griffin relocated to Silver Plume where Alice would grow up and fall in love with a local boy.

Jerry Buckley left his home state of New York for westward adventure. After a time, he settled in Silver Plume and went to work in the mines. In 1885, twenty-three-year-old Alice Griffin and Jerry Buckley were married in the Catholic church in Georgetown. Jerry built a small house for the couple on Water Street, facing Clear

Above: *This portrait of the Silver Plume baseball team shows four of the Buckley boys: Jeremiah (back row, second from left), Will (second row, first on left), Ray (second row, last on right), and Bob (sitting in front).*

Below: *In white aprons, two of the Buckley brothers stand in front of their store in Silver Plume, circa 1915–1930.*

PHOTOGRAPHS COURTESY OF DENVER PUBLIC LIBRARY, SPECIAL COLLECTIONS.

Creek at the time. Here, Alice gave birth to all thirteen of their children, eight boys and five girls.

When Jerry Buckley was killed in 1909, Alice faced her future with stoic determination. She gathered her children together, told them of her business plan, and gave each of her grown children a position and responsibilities. Each of the Buckley businesses did well, but it was the transportation business that endured the test of time. The older sons, Jeremiah and William, operated the transportation business from the family's livery stables. The younger boys all performed their chores in a joint effort for the family business.

While Alice oversaw the day-to-day operations, her daughters did the cooking and cleaning. This eventually led to Alice opening a boarding house for the local miners. The Buckley family businesses were a mainstay in Silver Plume and soon everyone was calling Alice "Ma."

As the businesses prospered, Ma Buckley bought the building where one of her sons, James, worked. The Newman Meat Market, at the corner of Main and Silver Streets, became the Buckley Brothers Building. The Buckley family operated a general store here until they outgrew the building and moved to a new location not far from the family home at the corner of Woodward Avenue and Water Street.

The Buckleys would eventually open the first Dodge dealership in the state and later opened a Studebaker dealership in Denver as well as a repair garage in Georgetown in 1920. After the Colorado and Southern Railway abandoned the line to Silver Plume, the Buckleys were awarded the mail contract. Jerry delivered the mail from Silver Plume to Georgetown and all areas in between until 1935. He missed only one day.[8]

For over forty years, Ma Buckley built her family business and instilled family pride in her children. Alice Griffin Buckley died in 1947 at the age of eighty-five. She was well respected in Silver Plume and known for her kindness.

Today, her descendants still carry on a few of the businesses Alice "Ma" Buckley created.

Notes

1. City Directory of Leadville, 1882.
2. Temple Israel Biographies, Newhouse.
3. The Argo Tunnel archives.
4. Dedman, James C. *History of Clear Creek County: Tailings, Tracks, and Tommyknockers.* The Historical Society of Idaho Springs, 1986. p. 292.
5. ibid.
6. ibid.
7. *History of Clear Creek County,* p. 217.
8. ibid.

3

THE SILVER BONANZA

LEADVILLE

THE SILVER BOOM at what would become Leadville was one of the West's most dramatic and important historical events. Almost overnight Leadville took the title of Colorado's mining capital away from Central City. The great riches that were unearthed from Leadville mines would establish the city as Colorado's most important industrial mining district for many years.

The rush of miners, tenderfeet, merchants, and fortune seekers who headed west during the Pikes Peak Gold Rush of 1858–1859 brought thousands to the area that would become Colorado Territory. They were known as the "'59ers," the pioneers who built and shaped the great state we enjoy today, which, through their political leadership and business foresight, resulted in Colorado gaining statehood in 1876. Through the direct cause and effect of the gold frenzy, ore mining became the number one industry in the state. As such, rich ore strikes occurred all over the state, from Central City to the San Juan mountain range, and from Creede to Leadville. The pioneers of the '59ers became the leading businessmen and politicians of the new Centennial State. The most notable of all was undoubtedly Horace Austin Warren Tabor and his wife, Augusta. Their silver saga produced millions, resulting in the highest town in Colorado, known as Leadville, the treasured mountain mining town in the clouds.

Twenty years after the gold rush, Colorado's silver boom sprang to life. In 1879, the lure of silver brought thousands more to the newly inaugurated Centennial State. Horace Tabor would become the state's first millionaire due to silver and thereby be crowned the "Bonanza King" of Leadville, if not all of Colorado. For Leadville is where it all happened and Tabor was at the forefront, as were both of his wives, Augusta and Baby Doe.

It was William H. Stevens, a name nearly lost to Colorado history, who actually led the first group of miners up the Rocky Mountains, to a place where the first silver riches were eventually found. It was Stevens who would figure out that the dark, dingy, slimy mud miners struggled to separate from the gold was actually a carbonate of lead rich in silver. But that would be fifteen years in the making. In the spring of 1860, Stevens and his group, which included Abe Lee, followed Bear Creek to the South Platte River, west through the South Park region, where they crossed the Mosquito Range near the present town of Granite. By April 1860, they had hit the Arkansas River, which led them to the valley and dry gulches between Colorado's highest peaks, 14,433-foot Mount Elbert and 14,421-foot Mount Massive. Here they followed a good-looking stream that yielded "color" in the water in a gulch crowded between Carbonate Hill and Rock Hill to the west. It was here that Abe Lee pulled from the river a pan full of gold, exclaiming, "Boys, I've got all of California in this here pan."

W. P. Jones' version, one of the first written of this discovery, holds a ring of truth, as he was actually present at the time. With Abe Lee's find, the area was called California Gulch. Miners swarmed to the area and soon the mining camp of Oro City came to be.

One of those miners was Horace A. W. Tabor. A tried and true '59er, Tabor brought his wife, Augusta, and infant son, Maxcy, to the gold riches of the Colorado Rockies following the original Gregory strike at Central City. After a few attempts at gold mining, particularly at Payne's Bar (Idaho Springs) where his claim was jumped, the Tabors moved higher into the hills, finally arriving in the Oro City settlement, such as it was, in the fall of 1860. While Tabor immediately began mining in the area, Augusta saw the advantage of business opportunities and opened a baking shop. So popular was her baking, not to mention the fact that she was the only woman in the camp, the miners built her a cabin, where she could expand her cooking skills for all the miners. Here the Tabor family stayed and helped build the community. Augusta would become postmistress and Tabor would be elected as the first mayor. The couple would go on to bring so much more to Leadville.

Silver and the town of Leadville sustained the state of Colorado through the slow economic times of the 1880s and produced business leaders and millionaires such as Charles Boettcher, David Moffat, the Guggenheim brothers, J. J. Brown and his wife, Molly, and John F. Campion, to mention a few.

Today, high in Rockies, the history and legacy of Leadville is very much alive.

Augusta Tabor, shown here circa 1885, had a strength of character that well suited her as the matriarch of Colorado pioneers. PHOTOGRAPH BY ALFRED E. RINEHART, COURTESY OF DENVER PUBLIC LIBRARY, SPECIAL COLLECTIONS.

Augusta Louise Pierce Tabor: Leadville's First Lady

Augusta Tabor was a grand lady, the matriarch of Colorado pioneers. The first wife of H. A. W. Tabor, married in 1857, Augusta was later abandoned by her beloved Tabor after he struck it rich in Leadville.

So much has been written of the Tabor "rags to riches to rags" story, or the love story between Horace and Baby Doe, and the infamous but untrue deathbed quote "Hang on to the Matchless, it will make millions," and the story of the great rise of H. A. W. Tabor himself, from a miner to high political office, scandal, and eventual ruin. Yet, with all the interest in the Tabor saga, one of the key players is nearly always left out: the complete story of Augusta Louise Pierce Tabor. Thanks to her love for journalism and newspaper reporters, she visited newspaper offices in both Leadville and Denver, and reporters were able to capture the true Augusta. Her Leadville friend, Alice Polk Hill, as well as Flora Bishop of Denver, wrote extensively on the life of Augusta. Most of those writings are preserved in Augusta's scrapbooks, housed at the Denver Public Library. Hill wrote a small booklet about Leadville and featured Augusta.

Born to William and Lucy Pierce on March 29, 1833, Augusta was named for the beloved city where the Pierce family resided in Maine. Augusta was the third daughter of the Pierces, who had eight children. As a child, her health was a constant worry and Augusta relied on pure determination to see herself through school. It was a hard-earned trait and one that would serve her well all her adult life.

In the summer of 1853, twenty-two-year-old Horace Tabor left his Vermont home to learn the stone-cutting trade. How he learned of William Pierce's stone-cutting business is unknown; nevertheless, Tabor showed up at the Pierce family–owned stone-quarry business in Augusta, Maine. Tabor, who came from a poor family in Vermont, was nevertheless ambitious and hardworking, something Mr. Pierce must have sensed, as he hired him straight away. It wasn't long before Tabor turned his eye toward the boss' daughter. Young Augusta was also smitten. Following a customary courtship, approved by Augusta's parents, Tabor proposed to Augusta and the two were married at Augusta's family home on January 31, 1857. Tabor was twenty-six years old, and Augusta was twenty-three. A Pierce family friend, Reverend John Ingraham, performed the service. Augusta later recalled, "On January 31, 1857, we were married in the room where we first met." [1]

During the two-year courtship, Tabor had taken out a homestead near Manhattan, Kansas. It must have been one of the biggest decisions of Augusta's life when she agreed to go west for her honeymoon and a new life. The newlyweds set their sights for the midwestern area of Kansas Territory. In May 1857, the couple struck out for the Republican River Trail, a lonely, desolate trail with alkaline water and very little wild game. Augusta wrote:

> I had to cook for the party, and I did not find it pleasurable. Sometimes the wind would blow furiously, and it is not very pleasant to cook over a campfire in a windstorm when the fire is made of Buffalo chips and every gust of wind would carry them over the barren prairie. By the time I would get them gathered together, another puff—and so on—lasting three or four days.[2]

Augusta must have been aghast when she saw her farmland. It was nothing like the rich, green, rolling hills of her beloved Maine or even Vermont. Here, in the windswept prairie of Kansas, Augusta must have felt as desolate as the land itself. At the meager homestead, Tabor built an equally meager log cabin. Augusta later described the scene: "The log cabin stood alone and solitary upon an open, wind-whipped prairie."[3]

Tabor didn't farm or raise livestock, although Augusta did, but he found work at nearby Fort Riley, primarily as a stone cutter. Augusta labored with the farm and took in boarders to supplement their income. In this way the Tabors were able to pay off the homestead and have a little money left over.

In October 1858, Tabor was away at work at Fort Riley when Augusta gave birth to their child. She named him Nathaniel Maxcy, after the man who had come west with them and had helped her through the childbirth.

Over the winter the Tabors heard about the rich gold finds in the Colorado Rockies. The stories were fantastic and even a bit too good to be true. But Horace was determined to go west and seek their fortune. When spring came, the Tabors, along with their friends Nathaniel Maxcy and Samuel Kellogg, prepared to leave Kansas behind for the glorious goldfields of Colorado. They rented out their farm and log cabin to William Shepard. The Tabors paid their creditors and were now free to go west. Augusta later recalled: "When those obligations were made, I as my husband's silent partner, a legal nonentity, with no voice or power for self-protection under the sun, but when penalty accrued, I was his legal representative."[4]

A young Nathaniel Maxcy Tabor poses in finery for a portrait. PHOTOGRAPH COURTESY OF DENVER PUBLIC LIBRARY, SPECIAL COLLECTIONS.

With their meager possessions tucked away in the wagon, baby Maxcy tucked in a warm blanket, Augusta took her place beside her husband as they began this new journey farther west. On May 5, 1859, the Tabor party set out on a long westward journey. Again, they chose the less-traveled Republican River Trail. The road was nothing more than a path for the cattle, with no visible lines for travel, so Horace gave them the lead. The men and Augusta soon fell into a routine. Every Sunday the men went to hunt wild game. Augusta was left behind to tend to the laundry, food preparation, and making the campsite comfortable, all the while looking after her infant son, Maxcy. Augusta later recalled: "On Sundays we rested—if rested it could be called. Mr. Tabor would go hunting while I would cook, wash and iron, which kept me employed all day. My baby was teething and was sick all the way across."[5]

After nearly two months, the weary travelers arrived at Denver City. It was June 1859. The sun was high in the sky with the promise of new beginnings. The Tabors were part of a very special group, the '59ers. Augusta's recollection of this time is a testament to her and the '59ers: "What I endured on this journey only the women who crossed the plains in '59 can realize. My babe was teething and suffering from fever and augue, so he required constant attention. I was weak and feeble. My weight was only ninety pounds."[6]

Because their horses were worn and their cattle were footsore, the Tabors and their traveling companions camped at the edge of Denver City, along the South Platte River, where the railroad yards are today. The men went into town and found news of the latest gold strike, gathering the information to make an intelligent and informed decision about when and where to strike out for their chance at a gold discovery.

On July 1, the group began climbing through the foothills of the Rocky Mountains. They were headed for John Gregory's Gregory Diggings. Following Clear Creek, they made their way to the spot where the future town of Golden would one day be. From the valley, these eager '59ers could see the steep, rocky incline of the mountain range before them. Leaving Augusta behind, the men headed up the mountainous terrain. For three long, lonely weeks, Augusta kept watch over her meager camp. An entry from her diary describes those early pioneer days:

> Leaving me and my sick child in the 7 x 9 tent, that my hands had made, the men took a supply of provisions on their backs, a few blankets, and bidding me be good to myself, left on the morning of the glorious Fourth, 1859. My babe was suffering from fever and I was weak and worn. My weight was only ninety pounds. How sadly I felt, none but God, in whom I then firmly trusted, knew. Twelve miles from a human soul save my babe. After three long weary weeks the men returned. On the 26th of July we again loded [*sic*] the wagon and started into the mountains. Traveling by way of Russell Gulch, it took us three weeks to reach Payne's Bar (Idaho Springs.) Ours was the first wagon through and I was the first white woman there, if white I could be called, after camping for three months."[7]

The men of the camp built a log home for Mrs. Tabor, the first in the camp known as Payne's Bar, today's Idaho Springs. Horace Tabor prospected for gold, while Augusta baked bread, pies, and sold meals to the miners. This was the beginning of Augusta's way of providing the main source of income for the family, a practice that would continue for twenty years, until Mr. Tabor's famous silver bonanza would be discovered near Leadville.

They did find their bonanza, and one would think life would forever be good. But that's not how it worked out, for either Augusta or Horace.

Augusta took in boarders, cooked meals, provided laundry services for the miners, sold baked goods, and eventually ran a general store, while Tabor dug for gold. Moving from mining camp to mining camp, from Idaho Springs to California Gulch to Buckskin Joe, Augusta was often the first white woman in the area, and her domestic services were a needed commodity.[8]

In February 1860, the Tabors headed south over Ute Pass and South Park. Augusta recalled her first look at South Park:

> I shall never forget my first vision of the park. The sun was just setting. I can only describe it by saying it was one of Colorado's sunsets. Those who have seen them know how glorious they are. Those who have not cannot image how gorgeously beautiful they are. The park looked like a cultivated field with rivulets coursing through, and herds of antelope in the distance.[9]

They trekked over snow, waded through rivers, and eventually made their way to Buckskin Joe. They built a small cabin where Augusta took in boarders while Horace prospected. To get the ore to an assayer or a local bank was a dangerous mission. Highway robbers lurked along the roads to Fairplay or Denver, waiting for a stagecoach to pass. In her book, *Cabin Life in Colorado,* Augusta recalled:

> I have been taken along as a body-guard a great many times when Mr. Tabor was going to Denver with treasure, because he thought he would not be so liable to be attacked. I have carried gold on my person many a time. He would buy all the gold that he could and we would carry it down ourselves rather than trust the express, because our express was often robbed. I have gone across the Mosquito Range with him on horseback. There we had no road at all. I had the gold in buckskins, then put in gunny bags, then laid on the horse and then my saddle put on over the blanket, and bring it that way. Then there would be nothing visible but the saddle. If anyone came along

> they would rather search him than me. There were some miles that we could not ride our horses on account of the wind, it blew so fiercely. We had to have our clothes tied on firmly. In some places it was so steep we had to hang on to our horses' tails, it was [all] the horses could do to get up.

Another incident of playing human decoy while transporting precious ore will be recounted in a subsequent chapter. The Tabors stayed in Buckskin Joe for seven years. Samuel Leach, another postmaster in the region, wrote a letter to his brother describing the Tabors and their general store and post office:

> We now have two mails a week to Denver by way of Buckskin Joe, as they call it here. I have to go there twice a week and fetch the mail bags over to this camp as it is in the cards for me to be the postmaster here.
>
> There is a postmistress at Buckskin Joe and I shall tell you about her. She keeps a boarding house and runs a store much like the one I am in charge of here. Her husband works in the mines. They are a young couple, about my own age, from down in Maine. He was a stone mason and worked for her father before they were married and during the time of their courtship he took up a homestead in Kansas. When they were married they went to Kansas to live and then crossed the plains and were in Denver, Idaho Springs and California Gulch for awhile. He has made some money and other investments. They are considered well to do here and they certainly are thrifty like the down eastern Yankees. She makes his shirts, put new bosoms in old ones, knits his socks, and makes her own soap. She is a good cook and the men like her pretty well although she is a driver.
>
> Well, I spent four evenings there in the last two weeks helping her sort out the mail. Then we played seven-up and high-five for a while and she often takes a hand. I like these people very well. Their name is Tabor; her name is August and his is Horace.[10]

Hearing of a new gold strike, in September, Horace took his family over Mosquito Pass and into California Gulch, where Abe Lee had washed just one more pan from the Arkansas River and given the gulch its name.

Following the usual pattern of moving from mining camp to mining camp, the Tabors stayed in California Gulch along the Arkansas River for quite some time. With the savings Augusta managed, the Tabors traveled to Maine later that summer and then returned to Colorado, as reported by the November 6, 1876, *Rocky Mountain News:* "Mrs. Tabor returned from the East with her husband. He is looking unusually well and full of animation and cordiality." Augusta related it was the happiest summer she remembered. It was not to last.

When the Tabors returned to Colorado, they learned a new boom was on. Silver! The heavy, black soil so cumbersome in mining for gold in California Gulch had been found to be full of silver and lead. The Tabors returned to California Gulch where a small mining community called Oro City had taken root. Augusta set up a mercantile store and post office. On November 30, Horace became postmaster and mayor of the mining town. Augusta and Lottie Williams, a schoolteacher and Augusta's friend, started the first school in the gulch and hosted a Christmas party for all the children.

The heavy black soil, however, still slowed the process and became quite a nuisance. Incredibly, the black sludge was discovered to be a carbonate of lead, the parent rock of silver! Samples assayed at two and a half pounds of silver to the ton. The miners, Tabor included, were stunned. That black dirt everyone had cussed was actually silver!

In the very year Colorado became a state, a new rush to the Rocky Mountains was on. Silver! The entire area swarmed almost overnight with miners in a frenzy to strike it rich. Before the year was out, $100,000 worth of silver came out of the first developed mine in California Gulch, and a new town was incorporated closer to the major mining claims. They called it Leadville.

The silver bonanza was on. As more and more silver was discovered in the heavy black soil of California Gulch, the miners, including the Tabors, moved upriver some two miles to Leadville. The well-known Tabors set up their general store at the corner of Harrison Avenue and Chestnut Street, where Augusta and Maxcy operated the store, as well as the post office, and Horace Tabor spent his time scouring for silver. When he and Augusta had saved $7,000, they hid it in the floorboards of the cabin.

Elected as the first mayor of Leadville in 1878, Tabor gained quite a name for himself. Now he spent more time in town, backslapping politicians and bankers, while making an occasional appearance in the Tabor general store. Yet, throughout the mining camp years, Horace's real gold mine was Augusta, who ran the general stores, operated the post office, and took in boarders all along the way, to further Tabor's dream.

Also, instead of prospecting for himself, Tabor occasionally agreed to grubstake miners, supplying them with the equipment and needed supplies in return for one-third of any silver discovery. On a fine day in May 1878, two miners looking for a grubstake walked into Tabor's store, and Tabor obliged a $64 grubstake. For nearly thirty days, August Rische and George Hook dug in the hills above Leadville, and then they struck a massive lode of silver on Fryer Hill. They immediately filed the claim, with Tabor's name included, and called it the "The Little Pittsburgh." In April 1878, Tabor received one-third of the richest silver strike to date in the state. The riches poured from the mine and soon Tabor bought out Rische and Hook for a song. With overnight riches reaching $10,000 a day, Tabor couldn't spend money fast enough. He bought up mining stakes all over the gulch, and all turned profits. Tabor was soon the richest man in Colorado. More and more of Tabor's mines became incredible successes, including the legendary Matchless Mine, and by the end of the decade Leadville literally was sewn in silver.

True to Tabor form, he began enriching the mining town of Leadville, the center of the richest silver strike in Colorado. Tabor started the first bank, founded a fire department, and within months began construction of a three-story brick opera house to be named in his honor. It was the grandest opera house west of the Mississippi River. All of this he accomplished within eighteen months of the rich silver strike.

And this was only the beginning. Within a year, the entire ore production for Lake County, of which Leadville was the county seat with Tabor as its mayor, was over $2 million. There were seventeen smelters, 500 businesses, and a population of 10,000. Tabor was reelected as mayor, and later that year he was elected lieutenant governor alongside Governor Frederick Pitkin.

Life was seemingly grand for the fabulously wealthy Tabors. Horace built a splendid two-story house for Augusta at 310 Harrison Avenue. The ever-frugal Augusta took in boarders to help defray the cost of the new home. Augusta's Leadville friends included Mrs. Helen Brumm, who came to Leadville penniless, took in washing, and ran a boarding house. There was also Mrs. Hannah Drifell, who, after the death of her husband, tried to mine but was forced to take in laundry to support her young children. And there was the flamboyant Mrs. J. J. Brown, whose husband was the superintendent of the Little Johnny Mine.

But now, because of Tabor's elevated status, the Tabors would have to move to Denver. In January 1879, Tabor rented and then purchased from Henry C. Brown his mansion at 17th and Broadway for $40,000. The home and grounds occupied the entire 1700 block of Broadway.[11] When Tabor took Augusta to see their new home, Augusta reportedly declared, "I will never go up these steps, Tabor, if you think I will ever have to go down them."

It wasn't that Augusta was against the finer things in life, as most have written about her. It was simply her pragmatic nature to budget for the finer things in life. On the other hand, her husband, with his newfound wealth, seemed to be buying anything and everything in sight without a care as to the future. Augusta saw this as foolish but did her part to please her husband, as the newspapers readily reported. On the evening of February 8, 1879, Augusta and her husband, the new lieutenant governor of Colorado, made their social debut on the Denver scene when they hosted a party for the state legislators and their wives in their new Broadway home. Flora Bishop, Augusta's dear friend whom she met during a visit to the offices of *The Rocky Mountain News*, later recalled the event, writing, "One thing pleasant I remember on this occasion was the presence of several older ladies, not in any way courted by society, but who had been her friends in former years, and whom she did not choose to ignore for newer if more elegant ones."

Flora Bishop and Augusta Tabor were indeed close friends. They were drawn to each other by their passion for writing. Up to this point, Augusta had only written in her diary and scrapbooks, but Flora encouraged her friend and soon Augusta was sending short articles about her ventures in the West to the local newspapers back home in Maine. Augusta's interest in writing prompted her to attend the annual convention of the Colorado Press Association held in Manitou Springs in July 1879. From *The Rocky Mountain News* dated July 13, 1879:

> At the ball at the Manitou house Wednesday evening, the ladies of the press club party wore some very pretty costumes. Mrs. H. B. Jefferies was attired in black silk with gold ornaments. Mrs. Governor Tabor, black silk with diamond jewelry. Miss Packard of Greeley, dove-colored and navy blue silk. Miss Higby, of Greeley, fawn-colored cashmere and satin. Mrs. Wolfe Londoner, pale blue lawn and white lace, with diamond ornaments. Mrs. W. E. Pabor, of Longmont, black lace and cashmere. Mrs. W. N. Byers, of this city, black bunting with claire de hue cape and fringe.

The August 18, 1879, issue of *The Rocky Mountain News* carried the following item: "Mrs. Governor Tabor, and her sister, Mrs. Clark, and her niece, Miss Susie Marston, of Leadville, are at the soda springs in California Gulch." Much of Denver society called on Augusta Tabor at her Denver mansion, including delegations from several churches, of which Augusta remarked, "I suppose Mr. Tabor's and my souls are of more value than they were a year ago." While Augusta kept up with appearances in Denver society,

Horace was buying more and more Denver businesses. He purchased part ownership in the Windsor Hotel, he bought shares in the First National Bank. He bought the Tabor Hose Company and Light Cavalry for the Denver Fire Department and bought the entire block of Larimer and Sixteenth Streets, where he intended to bring respectability to Denver. "Denver was not building as good buildings as it ought," he said, "and I thought I would do something towards setting them a good example."

Tabor was also building in Leadville. His massive Tabor Opera House was built of brick and said to be fireproof. It would command half a block on Harrison Avenue. To do this, the Tabor home had to be moved. When completed, it was a fine structure, with plush seats, low lights, and a commanding stage, complete with hand-painted backdrops. On the third floor, there was a walkway across the alley connecting to the Clarendon Hotel. Mysterious at the time, the purpose would eventually become clear. In the meantime, the press covered the Tabors' every move. The August 13, 1879, *Rocky Mountain News* reported, "Governor and Mrs. Tabor left yesterday morning for Leadville, to remain until September. Their many friends wish them a most pleasant sojourn in their old home. The Tabor hose will guard their interests here against fire and flood, meanwhile."

When opening night at the opera house came in late November 1879, Augusta took her place next to her husband in the elevated box seats. In July 1880, Augusta and Horace hosted former president and Mrs. U. S. Grant in their home. The Grants were guests of the Tabors at the opera house on July 23, 1880. Seated in the Tabor box, the two couples enjoyed the performance of "Ours." Later that evening, they attended a ball in the president's honor.

Despite these seemingly buoyant outings in Leadville society, there was gossip that the Tabor marriage was indeed not a happy one. And the gossip columns of the *Leadville Chronicle* certainly fanned the winds of gossip. "Mrs. Governor H. A. W. Tabor—in plum-colored brocade, point lace and diamond ornaments," the newspaper noted, "was escorted to a ball by Captain W. L. Thompson."

Apparently the paper sent a "detective" reporter to Denver to see what he could learn regarding the marriage of the Tabors. Two weeks later, the *Leadville Chronicle* reported, "The Denver Detective, of this week, has the following: 'There is much talk about Governor Tabor's family affairs.' It has often been stated that he and his wife have been divorced. This is not the case, for there is nothing on our county records to that effect. Mrs. Tabor stated to a lady friend that there was no truth in the rumor that the Governor had offered her $100,000 to give him a divorce. She said that she and Mr. Tabor had their differences, but that there had been no thought of separation."

In January 1881, however, Horace Tabor moved out of the Denver mansion and into a suite at the Windsor Hotel, where he was a part-owner. Augusta knew instinctively that there was another woman and had bought a third interest in the Windsor Hotel only a month prior to her husband's move. For the next few months, Augusta used her ownership of the hotel as an excuse to stop by on a regular basis. In fact, she was checking out the visitors to the hotel. And sure enough, a young blonde beauty was staying in the same suite as her husband. Her name was Elizabeth "Baby Doe."

Tabor had completed another Tabor Opera House, this one in Denver, and plans were being made for an opening night gala. The city intended to bestow a watch fob on Tabor for all he had done for Denver. There were also rumors that Tabor had his eye on a senate seat.

At the same time, Augusta was realizing a healthy monthly income from her Windsor Hotel investment and decided to take a trip abroad. When she returned, Augusta read the latest gossip about her husband in the newspapers and must have just cringed. She decided to do her part in rectifying the marriage. She penned a heartfelt and painful letter to her husband:

> Denver, September 3, 1881
>
> Dear Husband,
>
> I am in town and would like very much to go to the Tabor Grand and witness the Glory that you are to receive. Believe that none will be more proud of it than your broken-hearted wife.
>
> Will you not take me there and by doing so stop the gossip that is busy with our affairs.
>
> God knows that I am truly sorry for our estrangement, and will humble myself in the dust at your feet if you will only return. Whatever I said to you was done in the heat of passion and you know the awful condition that I was in when it was said. Pity, I beseech you and forgive me. And let us bury the past and commence anew. And my life shall be devoted to you forever.
>
> Your loveing, [*sic*] Wife [12]

Augusta's letter went unanswered. On opening night at the Tabor Grand Opera House, Tabor sat alone in his box. Somewhere in the vast audience sat the young and very beautiful Baby Doe.

Horace Tabor no longer wanted Augusta. He wanted Baby Doe as his wife. He offered Augusta $100,000 if she would grant him a divorce. Augusta looked at divorce as a shameful thing and a sign of defeat. Horace's gesture disgusted her. No divorce. She would fight for her marriage if not for her husband.

Tabor saw a different path to ridding himself of his wife. In January 1882, he traveled to Durango, the county seat of La Plata County. There he declared himself a citizen of the county and filed a complaint of divorce. How this could be and the fact that it was never served on Augusta is perhaps explained in one word—politics. Because of his former lieutenant governor status, Tabor was able to sway the county authorities into doing his bidding.

When Augusta found out, she was livid. It had come to this. Divorce. The news and the scandal were soon in all the papers. So be it. Augusta would fight back. She filed a bill of complaint in the Colorado courts, requesting not only alimony and maintenance, but half of Tabor's wealth as well. The entire legal complaint was reprinted in the *Leadville Herald* with the following reporter's commentary:

> An absorbing topic of conversation in the city during the past few days has been the difficulty between Hon. H. A. W. Tabor and his wife, and a correct copy of the complaint as filed in the suit is herewith presented: Augusta L. Tabor vs. Horace A. W. Tabor, complaint for alimony and maintenance.

The article went on to describe what Augusta and her lawyers deemed "their common, mutual exertions, patent industry, as well as acquired property, real, personal and mixed and economy for more than twenty-three years were valued at well over nine million dollars." Additionally, Augusta asked the court to declare the Denver mansion her sole and separate property and grant her the deed in her name only. For support and maintenance she asked for $50,000 annually. A small sum, given Tabor's massive wealth.

Gossip swirled in the Leadville wind. Was the pretty divorcée, Baby Doe, the reason for the Tabor difficulty and would Horace finally file for a legal divorce? How would this affect his political ambitions? And more secrets. It was soon learned that on September 30, 1882, Tabor and Baby Doe were secretly married in St. Louis, Missouri, following his Durango divorce.

Augusta's attorney, Amos Steck, used this illegal marriage against Tabor. In January 1883, Tabor and his attorneys agreed to Augusta's demands in her claim. She received the Denver mansion, several properties, and $50,000 annually. Horace received his divorce, and this time it was legal. In court, an anguished Augusta cried out, "Not willingly, Oh God, not willingly."

Shortly after the divorce proceedings, Tabor was asked to fulfill the thirty remaining days of Senator Thomas Bowen's term. Senator Tabor took Baby Doe to Washington, D.C., where an elaborate wedding took place. Now Tabor had his senatorship and his lovely bride at his side.

For Augusta, the divorce settlement left her very wealthy, yet heartbroken. For additional income, she took in boarders at her Broadway mansion, including her old friend, Flora Bishop. Her son Maxcy lived there as well, and this seemed to please Augusta. She immersed herself in social activities through the Unitarian Church and the Denver Women's Press Club and was dedicated to the Pioneer Ladies' Aid Society, helping needy women. Augusta continued her good work, as evidenced by a notice in the July 18, 1883, *Rocky Mountain News:* "A lawn party and social for the benefit of Unity church, will be given at the residence of Mrs. Augusta Tabor, on Broadway, next Friday evening. Elaborate decorations, a brilliant illumination, fine music, etc., may be expected." All the while, she managed to build on her assets in her typical frugal manner.

Augusta enjoyed traveling and did so often. Newspapers across the country seemed interested in the travels of Augusta Tabor. *The New York Sun* wrote, "A Colorado Lady [*sic*] who is said to be worth a million but who once was a cook in a miner's cabin, is now traveling in Europe, and has no agent or servants attending her. She attracts attention from her independent style." And from *The Rocky Mountain News,* dated January 31, 1881: "Mrs. H. A. W. Tabor will pay a visit to the Pacific coast very soon, accompanied by a party of friends."

Apparently, while she was away, her ex-husband and their partner, William Bush, were at odds and seemingly about to go to court. The *Leadville Chronicle* reported:

> Mrs. Augusta Tabor has returned from California, and went at once to her residence on Broadway. She looks much benefited by her visit to the Pacific slope, and seems in the best of spirits. A reporter called upon her to ascertain if she had anything to say of the trouble that had arisen between her former husband and Col. Bush.
>
> "I have simply glanced at the newspaper accounts of the affair and consequently am only partially informed as to the facts thus far developed. But it would be indelicate for me to say anything; and were I acquainted with every detail of the misunderstanding, I would have to decline giving out anything for publication."

In the lawsuit, Tabor accused Bush of embezzlement. Bush attempted to bring Augusta into the matter, according to the *Leadville Chronicle:*

> Mrs. Tabor is deeply mortified that the public prints should have indirectly connected her with business troubles between her husband and Col. Bush. The reporters have persistently attempted to interview her, it having been rumored that Col. Bush had visited her parlors within the past forty-eight hours and made a pretty strong talk, every effort of the press to induce the lady to discuss the matter has proved futile, and both Mrs. Tabor and her husband insist that she shall not be dragged into the controversy.

Augusta was succinct. "Well, there has been scandal enough, God knows," she said. "It would make a big volume if put in book form. It has aged me. Mr. Tabor used to be a truthful man. He has changed now." These comments, made to a Denver reporter, were the last Augusta had to say on the matter. After this public episode, Augusta kept to herself. She very quietly began investing in property. She purchased an apartment building, various parcels of land, including 120 acres near Westminster, Colorado, and a block of commercial property at Lawrence and Sixteenth Streets in downtown Denver.

Augusta now spent much of her time with her son Maxcy and his fiancé, Luella Babcock. She was quite fond of Miss Babcock and the two grew close. *The Rocky Mountain News* reported, "Mrs. H. A. W. Tabor, Miss Babcock and Rev. A. M. Weeks, of Denver, are visiting Leadville, and for the present are rusticating at Cottonwood Springs."

Another newspaper clipping, found in Augusta's scrapbook, from the *Denver Republican,* dated April 14, 1887, hints at something more: "Mrs. Augusta Tabor is re-fitting the Tabor mansion very elegantly in all the newest and latest styles of decorations and upholstery. It is thought that she will entertain a great deal this coming season." In fact, "re-fitting" the mansion was due to the upcoming wedding of her son and Luella Babcock. The *Leadville Chronicle* carried the story:

> The Denver wedding of special interest to Leadvilleites was that of Maxcy Tabor and Lou Babcock at 5 P.M. on Thursday, January 17, 1883, in the home of the bride's parents Mr. and Mrs. John Babcock. According to the Associated Press dispatch from Denver: The preparations were very elaborate. The list of invited guests included about ninety of the most intimate friends of both contracting parties, including ex-Senator and Mrs. H. A. W. Tabor,

> Mrs. Augusta Tabor and Mr. and Mrs. William Bush. The ceremony was performed by Rev. Dr. Reuben Jeffery and Rev. Dr. A. M. Weeks.
>
> After the reception the new Mr. and Mrs. Tabor departed for the east, and will go directly to St. Louis, from whence they will travel to the various eastern cities at leisure.
>
> A sensible gift was that of Mrs. Augusta Tabor, who presented the young couple with a handsome residence on California street. The property is in the vicinity of the Gilpin school, is a valuable one, and in every way fitted for a handsome and comfortable residence. The surroundings are good, and the house is large, roomy and provided with all the modern conveniences. It is eminently fitted for a home, and a mother's love is strongly apparent in the gift.
>
> It has been arranged that the young couple will occupy the Tabor mansion on Broadway, upon their return from the east. Mrs. Augusta Tabor will then be absent in Cuba, and the somber rich old house will furnish a fine background for the bright young faces which will there await her return sometime next summer.

The following summer was indeed a busy one for the Tabors. Augusta returned from her trip and was delighted to hear the news that Luella would soon be giving her a grandchild. Maxcy was now the manager of the Brown Palace Hotel and as such, he urged his mother to move into the hotel. Augusta leased out her Broadway mansion and moved across the street to the elegant Brown Palace Hotel. Later that year, Luella gave birth to a lovely baby girl, Persis Augusta.

By 1894, it was apparent to all that Augusta's health was failing. She suffered from numbing arthritis and respiratory ailments. On the advice of a doctor, Augusta went to California in search of a milder climate. She settled in at the Hotel Balmoral in Pasadena. However, her cough only worsened.

On January 30, 1895, Augusta Louise Pierce Tabor died. The cause of death was listed as chronic bronchitis. She was sixty-two years old. A small notice appeared in the *Denver Post* on February 4, 1895:

> **DEATH ANNOUNCED**
>
> N. Maxcy Tabor left Pasadena, California last night for this city with the body of his mother, Mrs. Augusta Tabor, who died on Friday morning. The funeral will occur late in the week.

Three days later, Maxcy arrived in Denver with the body of his mother and a funeral was arranged, as reported in the February 7, 1895, issue of the *Denver Post:*

> The funeral of Mrs. Augusta Tabor will be held tomorrow at 2 o'clock in the afternoon at Unity Church.
>
> Reverend N.A. Haskell will deliver the funeral sermon. Internment will be in the family plot at Riverside where Mrs. Tabor had laid to rest two brothers within a year.
>
> Maxcy Tabor arrived in California too late to see his mother alive, she having passed away on the day before. He is nearly overwhelmed with grief.

During the morning hours of February 8, Augusta's body reposed at the home of Frances Pierce at 2147 Grant Street. At noon, the body was taken to the Unitarian Church at Broadway and Nineteenth Streets. Augusta's beloved church was overflowing with loving mourners. A special section was reserved for the Pioneer Ladies' Aid Society, of which Augusta had been a devoted member.

In his eulogy, the Reverend N. A. Haskell said, "Her name will ever be associated with the history of this state and of this beautiful city."

Margaret Tobin "Molly" Brown: Ahead of Her Time

She was a product of Leadville's riches. This unconventional lady did things her way and opened doors for women who followed her. This is the story of Margaret Tobin Brown, another legendary lady of Leadville.

Margaret Tobin was born July 18, 1867, in the Mississippi River town of Hannibal, Missouri, the same town where Samuel Langhorne Clemens grew up and later wrote of his childhood experiences under the pseudonym Mark Twain. Her father, John, and her stepmother, Johanna, had a small home in the area known as Shantytown. John worked at the Hannibal Gas Works and Johanna managed the household, raised the children, saw to their education, and insisted on proper Catholic religious training.

Maggie, as she was fondly called by her family (she was never called Molly in her lifetime), went to work at the local Garth Tobacco Factory at the age of thirteen to help with the family's finances. The hours were long, and the work was dirty and required extensive physical labor. While Maggie worked hard at her job, six days a week, she hated it, but the strong work ethic stuck with her for the rest of her life.

Maggie's older half-sister Mary Ann and her husband, Jack Landrigan, left for Leadville in 1883. Three years later, Maggie and her older brother, Daniel, left on a westbound train for Colorado to join their sister. Arriving in Leadville, Maggie lived with her sister and brother-in-law, and quickly found employment at the Daniels, Fisher & Smith Emporium on Leadville's main thoroughfare of Harrison Avenue. Again, her hard work ethic proved to be her greatest asset and she became a valued employee.

On a pleasant, sunny Sunday, Maggie caught the attention of Leadville mining superintendent J. J. Brown.

James Joseph Brown, the son of Irish immigrants John and Cecilia Palmer Brown, was born in Waymart, Wayne County, Pennsylvania, on September 27, 1854. Following his schooling, he went to work in the Pennsylvania coal mines. In February 1877, at the age of twenty-three, Brown made his way west.

Brown first worked in the gold mines in the Black Hills of Dakota Territory. After two years, with a bit of knowledge and experience, he moved on to the silver mining area of Aspen, Colorado. It was here that he met influential mining men who would become lifelong friends. However, dissatisfied with a salary of four dollars a day, Brown, an intelligent and ambitious man, left Aspen for better opportunities. In 1882, he moved to Leadville, known as the "silver capital of the world." Brown found work in the local mines and at night he studied geology and mining technology.

His efforts paid off. In 1885, he was hired as a shift manager for a group of silver mines, known as Imex Mining Company, owned by David Moffat and Eben Smith. Deeper exploration was required, digging shafts into the earth and rock. Due to his knowledge, work ethic, and dedication, Brown was promoted to foreman and then superintendent of the Louisville, the Maid, and the Henriette Mines, which were some of the richest mines in Leadville. Over the next fourteen years Brown improved the mining technology and boosted the profits of his company. His reputation as a competent mining engineer became well known throughout the area. The *Leadville Herald Democrat* declared Brown as "one of the best mine superintendents in the district."

It was in the early summer of 1886 that he met a fiery blue-eyed, red-haired Irish Catholic lass by the name of Margaret Tobin. The two were in attendance at a picnic sponsored by the Church of the Annunciation. A whirlwind courtship soon began.

The courtship of J. J. Brown and Margaret Tobin began with a mutual interest in the theater, both often attending performances at the Tabor Opera House in Leadville. Long carriage rides and picnics followed. After a six-month courtship, the couple were married on September 1, 1886. The groom was thirty-one years old and the bride had just turned nineteen. The wedding ceremony took place in the Catholic Annunciation Church in Leadville, officiated by Leadville's respected pioneer Catholic priest, Father Henry Robinson. Among the many wedding gifts received was a splendid solid silver tea service from the miners of the Leadville mines.

The *Leadville Herald Democrat* reported the wedding nuptials with their high approval of the union in the September 2, 1886, issue:

> An event that commands a prominent place in the social and hymnal records of the year was the marriage of Mr. J. J. Brown, the popular superintendent of the Louisville mine, to Miss Maggie Tobin, the accomplished young saleslady for whom the patrons of Messrs. Daniels, Fisher & Smith's will invoke the richest blessings. The contracting parties are, in fact, both well-known to the good people with whom they have been cast in the Cloud City, and no two could elicit more sincere expressions of approval than those which have been listened to at this time.

Following the wedding, the couple lived briefly at 322 West 7th Street in Leadville. Later they moved closer to the mines where Brown worked, a small mining camp called Stumptown. Here the couple lived in a small two-room cabin near the Louisville Mine. It was a rugged existence. Water had to be pumped from the only well in the camp and then hauled back to their cabin. This was their home for the next few years. Over the years, Maggie loved to repeat a story from this time period. She said that one night J. J. came home late from the mine, with the mine's money in a box. To hide it, he put in the cookstove. The following morning, Maggie started a fire in the cookstove and a frantic J. J. appeared in the room. Maggie said all the money burned, the amount growing with each telling of the story. The reality is that if the incident were true, it would have been coin or bars and recoverable. No one in the Leadville mining town carried paper money at the time.

Maggie gave birth to their first child, Lawrence Palmer, on August 30, 1887. A daughter, Catherine Ellen, who was called Helen, joined the family on July 1, 1889. With a growing family, the Browns moved back into Leadville where they bought a modest clapboard house at 300 East 7th Street. Maggie began extensive tutoring sessions with Mrs. Wooster, where she was instructed in literature, art, and music. This was also about the time when Maggie's father and stepmother, John and Johanna, sold their home in Hannibal and moved to Leadville, bringing with them Maggie's

Even in her youth, Maggie Brown was equal parts bon vivant, social activist, and businesswoman. PHOTOGRAPH COURTESY OF THE LIBRARY OF CONGRESS, LC-USZ62-9403.

stepbrother William and stepsister Ellen. Maggie later wrote that these were the happiest years of her life.

Through J. J.'s mining connections, the Browns began hosting parties in their home. The couple soon became well established in Leadville's social circles, hosting gala balls and social benefits.

In 1891, the Ibex Mining Company was formed by several prominent Leadville mining men such as Eben Smith, August R. Meyer, A. V. Hunter, and John F. Campion, friends of J. J. Brown. Campion was well respected for his mining knowledge and was known as "Leadville Johnny." Many historians and writers have often confused J. J. Brown with "Leadville Johnny."

In 1893, Campion hired Brown as superintendent, to lead the development of their mines, including one in particular, known as the Little Jonny Mine. The silver mine was a rather small producer and had changed owners several times before Campion and his company purchased it. The original discoverer, John F. Johns, named his mining claim for his son, Johnny. However, the recorded mining claim left off the "h" in "Johnny."

Campion and Brown were well suited to work together. They were the mining men of the new era. The days of surface mining were over. To find the richer ores, mine owners needed to devise ways to dig deeper into the earth. Brown was given the task of finding a way into the depths of the Little Jonny Mine. For the next few years the two worked together, devising methods, utilizing technology, and experimenting.

Brown ordered an additional mine shaft to be dug at the Little Jonny. However, the shaft hit a layer of dolomite sand, which caused the vertical shaft to cave in. Brown's persistence and experimentation paid off. He used bales of hay and added timbers to stabilize the walls of the shaft. The digging continued, eventually pushing through the sand and opening the lower area of the mine. There, a treasure trove of vast quantities of copper and gold were discovered. Brown and his employers turned the former silver mine into a gold mine, producing more gold than the Leadville area, known for silver, had ever seen.

"Little Jonny Strike to Revive Leadville." This was the October 29, 1893, headline of the *Leadville Herald Democrat*. The article went on to report that the Little Jonny Mine was shipping more than 135 tons of gold ore per day and also noted that Colorado School of Mines' Professor Tilden had visited the mine and stated, "It is practically a lake of ore, with some of the vugs yielding as high as $60 to the pound in gold." It would prove to be Leadville's richest gold mine to date.

In 1893, the government repealed the Sherman Silver Purchase Act, which had allowed for silver as a monetary backing to the U.S. dollar. The country fell into a severe economic depression. With the silver mining industry being one of the state's major economic contributors, Leadville and other Colorado mines were particularly affected. Several mines across the state closed down nearly overnight, and many who had made their fortunes in silver went broke. Conversely, the price of gold, now the only metal ore backing the country's currency, rose to enormous prices. The rich gold vein found at the Little Jonny Mine saved Leadville mining. The following year, the Ibex Mining Company did so well that they paid $1 million in stockholder dividends. Grateful to J. J. Brown, the company awarded him with not only his share of the dividend, but an additional 12,500 company shares.

Now, with new wealth, Margaret Brown could pursue her interests. The rich couple moved to Denver, where they bought a splendid mansion at 1340 Pennsylvania Street, just blocks from downtown. J. J. remained involved in Leadville mining and often the couple traveled to Leadville. From a Leadville dispatch reporter, printed in the *Denver Times,* October 11, 1900:

> Mr. and Mrs. James J. Brown, formerly of this city and now of Denver, are guests of the Vendome hotel. Mr. Brown likes to get back to Leadville ever so often and meet with his old mining friends. Mrs. Brown, whose immense wealth has enabled her to travel the world, is still inclined to enjoy the life of the mining camp, and was greatly interested in hearing about the advancements made in the mining industry here in Leadville.

Because of her wealth, Maggie could afford to devote much of her time to charity work, having been snubbed by Denver society and the haughty "Sacred 36" (a group of the most elite women). Politically, Maggie supported many human causes, including the rights of women and children. From the *Denver Times*, May 12, 1899:

> **Fair Opens**
>
> Governor Thomas and Mayor Johnson opened the St. Joseph's hospital benefit bazaar at Coliseum hall last night. The hall was crowded. The exclusively fashionable element, the club women, the church aid societies, and even Dean Hart are in charge of the evenings which will intervene between now and the 20th inst., when the fair closes. The moving power in the whole scheme is Mrs. J. J. Brown, the president, whose organization of the various committees who have carried the undertaking up to its present dimensions, has been remarkably successful.

In opposition to her mine-owner husband, Maggie also supported the rights of miners. Following the horrific labor strike at Ludlow, where eleven women and children were killed, Maggie made her way to the site, where she set up hospital tents and donated money for medical supplies.

In time, J. J. could no longer tolerate his wife's suffragette manner. The lively woman he had married had gained a confident air that baffled J. J.'s standard concept of a wife. In 1909, after twenty-three years of marriage, J. J. and Maggie filed for legal separation. Staunch Catholics, they never divorced, but their separation was swift and final.

Soon after, Maggie rented out her Denver mansion and sought solace with her friends in the East, at Newport Beach. Then she traveled to Europe to visit her daughter, Helen. In April 1912, Maggie received an urgent cable from her son in the States. Maggie's grandson was gravely ill, and she booked the fastest passage available to return home.

On April 10, 1912, Maggie boarded the RMS *Titanic,* the finest ocean ship in the world. The maiden voyage of this great ship had been highly advertised. Maggie found herself in the company of the rich and powerful members of both American and European society. She dined with the Astors, the Guggenheims, and Bruce Ismay, the owner of the White Star Line and the *Titanic.*

But the ocean crossing didn't go as planned. Maggie's heroics in the face of disaster as the great *Titanic* sank are shadowed only by Maggie herself. While Maggie enjoyed telling occasional tall tales, she rarely discussed this tragic event or her part in organizing the survivors and the ultimate rescue. Maggie later stated she was never really frightened, yet true to her character, she immediately took charge. Concerned for several hysterical women hovering on the deck, Maggie gently encouraged them toward the lowering lifeboats. At 12:55 A.M., Maggie herself was forced into lifeboat number 6. In the darkness, with the stars dancing brightly overhead, Maggie calmed the women and encouraged them to row away from the sinking ship. After six hours of constant rowing, the lights of the SS *Carpathia* came into view and rescue was at hand. Safely aboard the *Carpathia,* Maggie made a list of the survivors' names and arranged to have them wired to the States. She formed a committee to help the destitute survivors and offered money of her own.

Following the rescue, Maggie's true character and compassion was finally exposed to all the world. With newspaper reporters and photographers hounding her, she bellowed, "Leave me alone, I have work to do. People need me. Come back later." And they did. She was photographed in New York with the crew of the *Carpathia,* and she set up a charity for the survivors of the *Titanic.*

Returning to Colorado, Maggie's brief moment in the national spotlight allowed her to further her causes. Spending her remaining years in New York and Denver, she worked hard for the suffragist movement and helped bring women's rights to the national forefront.

Maggie did travel to Leadville from time to time, usually around Christmas when she enjoyed putting on Christmas events for the children, contributing money, toys, and clothing. She was remembered as a kind, stately woman who enjoyed visiting with shop owners on Harrison Avenue.

Maggie even ran for Congress, based on her advocacy for equal rights. Although she did not win the election, she was one of the

Despite her misadventure on the SS Titanic, *Maggie Brown continued to sail across the Atlantic, here in 1930.* PHOTOGRAPH COURTESY OF DENVER PUBLIC LIBRARY, SPECIAL COLLECTIONS.

first women in the nation to take the bold step into male politics. During World War I, she went to Europe and organized nurses and other medical workers to care for wounded soldiers, winning the praise of the French. In 1922, her estranged husband died, leaving a complicated estate that took years of wrangling in court to settle. Then, on October 28, 1932, sixty-five-year-old Maggie Brown passed away in her sleep in New York City.

Brown was inducted into the Colorado Women's Hall of Fame in 1985, and her home in Denver's Capitol Hill neighborhood is today a popular museum. Leadville's Margaret "Maggie" Tobin Brown was truly a lady ahead of her time.

Nellie Madeleine Davis: Leadville's First Female News Editor

Her friends and family called her "Nellie." Folks around Leadville described her as pretentious, beautiful, and full of fun. When she came to Leadville as a child, she had no idea that one day she would run the town's most popular newspaper and become a great influence.

Carlyle Channing "Cad" Davis left his job as a printer at the *Denver Tribune* for Leadville in 1878. After settling his wife, Martha, and two daughters in a rented home, Davis and partners James Burnell and John Arkin set up shop. It was a twenty-five-foot by sixty-six-foot "sagebrush covered lot" for $175 on Harrison Avenue. They ordered paper, presses, and other materials, which were hauled from Colorado Springs over the mountain passes and arrived on January 6, 1879. On January 29, 1879, the first edition of their paper, *The Chronicle,* was published, with 500 copies selling for ten cents each. Before the week was out, retail sales *and* street sales totaled nearly 9,000 copies. Boys were hired to deliver papers door-to-door, and within six months *The Chronicle* was averaging 2,000 papers sold daily. The paper would take on different names such as *The Daily Chronicle* and the *Leadville Evening Chronicle*.

Unable to join the Associated Press, Davis hired a reporter in Denver and received news dispatches telegraphed over Mosquito Pass. Davis and his paper would also face stiff competition from W. A. H. Loveland's *Daily Democrat* and H. A. W. Tabor's *The Republican* newspapers.

Meanwhile, little Nellie was attending Leadville schools and enjoying herself in various activities including singing in the church choir, acting in school plays, and attending social events. Of course, her father was sure to feature his daughter's adventures in his newspaper, such as this note in the August 28, 1880, edition of *The Chronicle:*

> A children's entertainment is always delightful, but the performance given by the home juvenile Pinafore company in the parlors of the hotel, last evening was so excellent and very meritorious throughout that scarcely too much can be said in its praise.
>
> The children who took part are all under 12 and have been trained to perfection that reflects the greatest credit upon them and their leader, Miss Florence O'Brian.
>
> The cast, chorus, etc., included Lottie and Eva Schloss, Clara Major, Nannie Cass, Ella Smith, Jessie Lawrence, Madge Miller, Flora Leonard, Onie Parsons, Mattie Smith, Amie and Ida Caskell, Louise White and Nellie Davis.

It must have been quite fun for Nellie to grow up in Leadville where her father was the newspaper man. When she wasn't in school plays or the choir, Nellie enjoyed being with her father and learning the newspaper business. The two attended a social event that was covered by *The Chronicle* in 1882:

> **HIGH TEA LAST EVENING**
>
> A pleasing episode in the social history of Leadville and one that has been in joyful anticipation for some weeks past, occurred last evening at the elegant residence of Captain and Mrs. Jacque, on Third street west. The event is classified as a "High Tea" and for all that goes to make up a truly fashionable gathering of society people it probably never was equaled here. Instead of the guests being seated at one or two large tables, they found their places at a "bakers dozen" of small tables. There were twenty-three women and twenty-two men, with C. C. Davis and his daughter, Nellie, at the same table as Mrs. J. B. Grant, Mrs. Goodell and daughters Mary, Jennie, Kittie and Ollie.

After giving the seating arrangements for the other tables, the reporter described the menu, which included oysters on the half shell, trout, quail, shrimp salad and stuffed tomatoes, macaroons, and ladyfingers.

It was about this time that Nellie's father, Cad Davis, won the newspaper war with rival Loveland of the *Democrat* and Tabor of the *Republican*. He purchased both papers and consolidated them in his publishing company as the *Herald Democrat,* along with *The Chronicle.*

The Davis family celebrated Christmas that year by attending a Christmas dinner at the home of Mr. and Mrs. W. R. Owen. *The Chronicle* covered the story in this way:

> Mr. and Mrs. W. R. Owen, at their elegant home on East Eighth street, entertained at dinner Col. Chapin and wife Jessie, Capt. Jacque and wife and Frankie, C. C. Davis and wife and Nellie, Miss Jennie Goodell and Mr. H. B. Reynolds. A feature of the elaborate and elegant repast consisted of beautiful hand-wrought dinner cards from the pencil of the charming hostess. Mrs. Goodell and Mr. and Mrs. Grant did not come up to Leadville from Denver until later in the week.

Nellie seemed to enjoy her childhood in Leadville, as the following article from *The Chronicle* recounts in spring 1883:

> Miss Nellie Davis celebrates her tenth birthday this afternoon, with a party for her juvenile friends. about thirty-five assembled to wish her many happy birthdays. As the invitations particularly requested, 'no presents.' The little ones were in the best spirits, and the arrangements of the fresh flowers which adorned Miss Nellie's home harmonized well with the sweet faces and lovely costumes of the little guests. At the appointed time the little ones were ushered into the dining room, where a feast had been prepared. The usual birthday cake with ten candles occupied a conspicuous place on the table. They all seemed to enjoy themselves very much. The invited guests were as follows: Katie Wood. Nonia Wood, Lilla Wood, Ethel Rucker, Alice Fisher, Essie Fisher, Blanche Dougan, Jennie Conant, Daisy Mater, Josie Mater, Eaton Goodell, Frank Jacque, Mary Fornia, Norman Estey, Ethel Breen, Herbert Spooner, Harold Plater, Annie Londoner, Blanche Londoner, Esbie Bissell, Jacqueline Chatfield, Bessie Campbell, Georgie Bissell, Lula Loker, Nannie Loker and Ella Smith.

Nellie's father clearly enjoyed printing articles about his daughter over the years as she was growing up. One wonders how Nellie felt about it. Nellie took a real interest in the paper during her high school years until her graduation in 1893. Following graduation, Nellie attended St. Mary's College in Notre Dame, Indiana, graduating in 1895. A new social fad, color teas were all in vogue and Leadville was not to be outdone. One such tea was given in honor of the young ladies going away to school.

> A Green Tea was given by Miss Cora Smith and Misses Lotta and Eva Schloss. The Misses Jennie Patrick. Mollie Flitner, Ada Pemberthy, Kate Sweeney and Nellie Davis will leave in early September for Notre Dame, Indiana.
>
> — *The Leadville Chronicle*

Right: *Nellie posed for her yearbook in 1895 at St. Mary's College in Indiana, but she was already looking forward to life—and a career—back in Leadville.* PHOTOGRAPH COURTESY OF CUSHWA-LEIGHTON LIBRARY, ST. MARY'S COLLEGE.

Class of 1895— Back row, left: Agnes Ryan, May Hamilton, Louise Holmes, Madeline Davis, Maude Nichols
Middle row: Nellie Moore, Corinne Gray, Marjorie Brady, Mary Wagner, Nettie Wurzburg
Front row: Mary Burns, Emma Burns, Mary Doening, Anne Tormey, Minnie Ruppe

Following her graduation, Nellie returned to Leadville in the summer of 1895 to find her father had fallen ill. Twenty-two-year-old Nellie wasted no time in taking over her father's newspapers, seeing to the day-to-day operations, and becoming the editor of his combined daily papers. The following year, Leadville hosted the spectacular Ice Palace events all around town, centering on the large palace made of ice by locals. At this time, as Nellie was covering this event, the Colorado Press Association held its annual convention in Leadville. To Nellie's surprise and delight, she was elected vice president of the esteemed organization. From the *Leadville Chronicle*:

> This afternoon, the Colorado Press Association held its annual meeting in the Ice Palace's ballroom. Among the officers elected was Nellie M. Davis as second vice-president. She had taken over the responsibilities of the Herald Democrat and Chronicle after her father C.C. Davis, had suffered a breakdown in July of 1895.

Her father, meanwhile, moved to Southern California and by 1899 had started a newspaper there, the *Santa Barbara Herald*. He also penned a number of books, including an amalgam of history and autobiography, *Olden Times in Colorado*.

Although Nellie enjoyed working with newspapers, her first love was acting. She enjoyed traveling across the country appearing in plays from time to time. After a year of running the papers, Nellie sold them to the Leadville Publishing and Printing Company and departed Leadville for adventures in the theater. By all accounts, including this from the *La Press* of Montreal, Canada, Nellie was a huge success:

> Miss Nellie Madeleine Davis filled the leading role in which she again employed brilliant qualities which have made her a favorite here. She possesses an extraordinary degree of two great qualities—grace and naturalness. She plays with an admirable simplicity, and it is precisely this reason why she is so appreciated.

When America entered World War I, Nellie enlisted as a nurse and was soon off to France with the American Ambulance Corps. Following the war, she received the Croix de Guerre and Bronze Star for her service. The Leadville newspapers covered the return of their Doughboys with enthusiasm, including their girl, Nellie Davis. The *Herald Democrat* reported:

> She came to France from the United States of America and since the beginning of the war has constantly served in hospitals as nurse until her arrival at Soisons canteen, where she displayed a beautiful courage under bombardment. Miss Nellie Madeline Davis has a right to wear the war cross with a bronze star.

Of her Leadville days, the reporter wrote:

> Miss Nellie Davis is a Leadville girl, having lived her girlhood here and been a pupil for a number of years at the local schools. While her father, C. C. Davis, was owner of the *Herald Democrat,* she took charge at one time during his absence and managed the paper for several months.

Following the war, Nellie traveled to Algiers with the French Colonial Administration, serving as a relief nurse. Unfortunately, she contracted an illness that progressed and turned into paralysis. Nellie Madeleine Davis died on May 31, 1924, in Algiers, where she was buried. Yet her heart will forever be with her childhood home in Leadville.

Laura Evans: A Champion for the Miners

Leadville is a town of legends and Laura Evans was no exception. Miss Laura loved to have a good time. She lived life to the fullest and had a "devil may care" attitude. A few of her rollicking good times included a little horseplay, literally. Laura watched the horse-drawn chariots roll into Leadville when the Ringling Brothers brought their circus act to town. She and another parlor house girl conspired to rent a chariot and a couple of horses by giving the water boy a generous tip. The next thing Leadville knew, a horse-drawn chariot was speeding out of control, turning onto State Street, charging past the parlor houses and cribs, and then turning down Harrison Avenue, Leadville's main street. Laura tried to round a corner off Harrison Avenue too fast, hit a pole in front of the Vendome Hotel (originally H. A. W. Tabor's hotel), and the chariot tumbled over. As the chariot turned on its side, witnesses gasped as a harried Laura Evans tumbled out onto the street. The police were in the process of arresting her and her cohort, when a well-known businessman, and a customer of Laura's, intervened.

Laura Evans had become a true legend in her own time. She was very secretive about her upbringing, perhaps because her father was involved with the Ku Klux

Klan in her hometown of Mobile, Alabama.[14] Laura Evans was born May 31, 1874, and married at seventeen years old, then left her husband and daughter, and headed west for a new life. She changed her name and settled in St. Louis, Missouri, where she entered the world of prostitution. She was in her late twenties when she arrived in Denver, finding work on Market Street (originally known as Holliday Street).

By the 1890s, she was a well-respected madam when the horror of a murderous Jack-the-Ripper copycat known as the Denver Strangler left dead bodies up and down Market Street. Laura promptly left Denver for Leadville and the silver boom. As Laura later said, "The reason I left Denver when I did was that Jack the Ripper was ripping the wombs out of the girls on Market Street."[15]

In Leadville, Laura really made a name for herself. In the winter of 1896 Laura and her parlor house friend, Spuddy, wreaked havoc at Leadville's Ice Palace. The Ice Palace was built as a tourist attraction, at a cost of over $200,000—a lot of money in those days only to melt away come springtime. According to Laura, "It was the warmest winter they ever had." In any case, Laura had the notion to pull her horse-drawn sleigh right into the palace. As the horse and sleigh entered the palace, Laura tried to bring her horse, Broken Tail Charlie, to a halt.[16] The loud music inside the palace, echoing off the ninety-foot ice pillars, startled the horse, which began prancing and kicking. Laura recalled years later:

> I drove the sleigh inside the Ice Palace and knocked down some displays. He [the horse] kicked the hell out of our sleigh and broke ice shafts as he ran away. He kicked a four foot ice pillar all to pieces and ruined all the ore exhibits before he ran home to his stable.

Despite these escapades, it was not long before Laura was known for her skills with a horse. Later that same year, Laura became a heroine and true legend in Leadville. A strike had occurred at one of Leadville's many mines, the Maid of Erin. Armed union troops guarded the area and blocked the road from any non-union member. The owners, in an effort to get the payroll to the workers who chose not to strike, asked Miss Laura to smuggle the payroll through the union lines. Laura secured the payroll pouch in her bustle, beneath the layers of her skirts, mounted her horse sidesaddle, and rode up Carbonate Hill. As most men knew Laura from her State Street parlor house, she simply smiled sweetly and explained she wanted to visit a friend who hadn't been allowed to leave the mine on account of the strike. The guards let her pass and she safely relayed the payroll to the superintendent.[17] As Laura later told the story:

> I put the money in my bustle. You oughta seen me sewing up that thing. I had a beautiful grey corduroy riding habit up in Leadville and went up there [to the mine]. They thought I was perfect. And there were the soldiers. Great big muskets. I jumped off the horse and went inside the office. I pulled out the bustle, dropped on his desk, straightened my bustle and got on my horse. Well, for a bluff, it sure worked. Then they started shooting. I was too fast for 'em.[18]

Laura later recalled the owner was so grateful, as the payroll broke the strike, that she was asked to dinner at the owner's home. When she arrived at the dinner party, she was introduced as a business associate and discreetly given a $100 dollar bill as she left.

Although Laura helped break the strike, the miners quit coming around and her business suffered. Although high spirited to a fault, for all her pranks, follies, and daredevil rides, Laura Evans possessed a strong and serious nature. Despite her chosen profession, or because of it, Laura had confidence and a strong will unmatched by any other woman in the profession. She has been described as kind and generous, strict and calculating. She rolled her own cigarettes and kept her money in her stocking. She had a great sense of humor and a colorful manner, and at times her language equaled any miner's use of four-letter words. It is said she was quite a beauty in her younger days. Her dark eyes remained clear and twinkling throughout her life.

Laura Evans enjoyed life, including animals like her dog, Mr. Pimp Powers, and friends. PHOTOGRAPH COURTESY OF HISTORY COLORADO, H.6093.7.VI.

Laura Evans died on April 4, 1953. True to the end, she died as she had lived, on her own terms. And her legend lives on today.

Baby Doe McCourt Tabor: Leadville's Silver Queen

The years in Central City had been hard on Baby Doe. She desperately hoped to change that in Leadville. Arriving in the summer of 1880, Baby Doe planned to work for her friend Jacob Sandelowsky in his new clothing store on Harrison Avenue. Jake had come to Baby Doe's aid time and time again, in Central City and now in Leadville.

The trip to Leadville had been long and stressful for Baby Doe and Jake. It was a sixty-five-mile journey by stagecoach over steep mountain roadways and switchbacks over high mountain passes, following Ten Mile Creek. When they arrived in the bustling mining town, Baby Doe found a place to stay at a rooming house on Fifth Street, just off Harrison Avenue. The 1880 census lists her there, as a divorcée, under the name of "Baby Doe McCourt."

Jake, in partnership with Sam Pelton, immediately set up his new clothing store, ironically in the ground-floor showroom of the Tabor Opera House. Not only was Tabor Jake's landlord, but also a business partner in two mines. Jake had shortened his name to "Sands," and his store was known as Sands and Pelton's One Price Clothing Store.[19] At Jake's urging, Baby Doe began to work in the clothing store.

Before long, Baby Doe knew all the gossip about town. Most of it concerned Tabor, his riches, and his political power. Curious, Baby Doe asked Jake for an introduction. One evening in the spring of 1880, while Baby Doe and Jake were dining at the Clarendon Hotel next to the Tabor Opera House, Horace Tabor entered the room with his partner, William Bush, who was Baby Doe's friend in Central City.[20] It is safe to say that Baby Doe was awestruck and Horace was smitten. Horace invited Baby Doe and Jake to join him at his table. Soon, Baby Doe set her sights on Horace and he on her. Tabor was forty-nine years old, while Baby Doe was just twenty-five.

Horace moved Baby Doe into a suite at the Clarendon Hotel, next to his opera house. In this way, he could leave the opera house and discreetly use the third-story walkway that connected to Baby Doe's rooms. Horace was the lieutenant governor of Colorado and as such, it would be a terrible political scandal if their trysts ever came to light. Now, Baby Doe had inserted herself into those very rumors swirling around Leadville. But the Leadville press never wrote a word.

In January 1881, Horace officially ended his marriage to his wife, Augusta, when he moved out of their Broadway mansion in Denver and into a suite at the Windsor Hotel. In no time, Horace moved Baby Doe from Leadville to Denver and into

When Horace Tabor began romantically pursuing Baby Doe, he was nearing fifty years old and she was half his age. BABY DOE PHOTOGRAPH BY ALFRED E. RINEHART; BOTH PHOTOGRAPHS COURTESY DENVER PUBLIC LIBRARY, SPECIAL COLLECTIONS.

his suite at the hotel. Horace was in the midst of completing his mark on Denver; his massive $800,000 Tabor Block, which included businesses and the Tabor Opera House. He invited Baby Doe to join him when he picked out the upholstery, curtains, and wallpaper. The couple delighted in the latest fashions: golden light fixtures, velvet draperies, and matching velvet-covered chairs. However, on opening night, Tabor sat alone in the Tabor box. Baby Doe was lost somewhere in the audience. Inscribed on the closing curtain was a quite prophetic quote from Charles Kingsley: "So fleet the works of men, back to the earth again. Ancient and holy things fade like a dream."

Augusta refused to grant Horace a divorce, so he and Baby Doe went to Durango where Horace paid a judge to grant him a divorce. Then he and Baby Doe were secretly married on September 30, 1882, in St. Louis, Missouri. In time, the secret divorce came to light and was proven to be illegal. The divorce from Augusta was ugly and costly. Horace gave her the Broadway house and another property, worth a total of $500,000. Finally, a defeated, tired Augusta relented. It was January 1883, a new beginning for Horace.

That same month he lost his election bid to become a U.S. senator but was invited by his party to serve out the remaining thirty days of Senator Henry Teller's term. Tabor was sworn in on February 3, 1883, in Washington, D.C. He would serve as senator until March 4. Elated, Horace took Baby Doe with him to Washington, where he threw the biggest, most elaborate wedding the city had ever seen. Invitations were engraved in silver leaf and even President Arthur attended. The wedding and dinner were held at the elegant Willard Hotel on March 1, 1883. Baby Doe McCourt was adorned in a $7,000 white silk dress accented with a $75,000 diamond necklace, a gift from the groom. It is said the largest diamond in the set had once been part of Queen Isabella's jewels. The wedding was both the event and the scandal of the season. Nevertheless, Baby Doe became Mrs. H. A. W. Tabor, legally this time.

Back in Colorado, everything Tabor touched seemed to turn to gold (or silver, as it were). He bought mines with names like the Matchless, Chrysolite, Maid of Erin, and the Little Pittsburgh. All made millions. The combined income from the mines alone was $2 million annually. In Denver, he bought a half interest in the First National Bank, mines in Aspen, forests in Honduras, and real estate as far away as Chicago, Illinois. Tabor just got richer and richer and so did his wife.

Their first home was located at 1647 Welton, a brick two-story with a large porch, but Tabor wanted something bigger, much bigger. In 1886, Tabor bought a large mansion on Capitol Hill for $54,000. The property ran the entire block of Thirteenth Street on the south side of Sherman Street. A large brown stone wall surrounded the property where Baby Doe had nude statues placed on the grounds. The Tabors had three carriages and six horses, two sets of pure white horses (Baby Doe's favorite), two coaches, and two footmen. When Baby Doe would go out, she would choose the carriage, either black, brown, or blue that best matched her dress.

When General William Tecumsah Sherman made a tour of Colorado mines, Tabor hosted him in Leadville. Tabor and Baby traveled from Denver to Leadville in David Moffat's private railroad car on the South Park Railroad line. Tabor met the general at the Clarendon Hotel and proceeded to give him a grand tour of Leadville's silver mines. Following dinner at the hotel, the general was a guest in the Tabor box at the Tabor Opera House. The box was simply stunning that night. Chilled champagne was served. Fresh lilies adorned the area, Baby's favorite flower. That was a custom Tabor arranged whenever Baby was in attendance, both in Leadville and Denver.

The Tabor's first child, Elizabeth Bonduel Lillie Tabor, was born on July 13, 1884. She was blonde and fair, and the picture of her mother. Tabor had gold medallions made with the inscription "Baby Tabor" and the birth date on one side and "Compliments of the Tabors" on the other. The Tabors traveled to Baby's hometown of Oshkosh for the christening. The baby girl was adorned in a pure silk christening dress fastened with gold pins and inlaid diamonds. It was a $15,000 affair. No matter. The Tabor mines were producing over $80,000 a month.

The king and queen of Leadville silver were treated like royalty and were living like it as well. The following summer the *Fairplay Flume* reported the Tabors were in town: "On Tuesday the Gilman House at Como was livened up by the presence of Mr. and Mrs. H. A. W. Tabor, who were en route to Leadville. Mrs. Tabor, nee McCourt, shone resplendent in silk and diamonds."

A son, Horace Joseph, was born on October 17, 1888, but he lived only a few hours. A second daughter, Rose Mary Echo Silver Dollar Tabor, was born to the couple on December 17, 1889. Baby called her "Honeymaid." She had dark hair and resembled her father. As she grew, her temperament was also a match for her father's.

In January 1887, two-year-old Lillie Tabor's picture was featured on the front cover of *Harper's Bazaar* magazine. It was a lovely sketch by Thomas Nast. The Tabors were proud parents indeed. The doting parents lavished gifts on their beloved daughters. Ponies, silk dresses, and expensive toys were enjoyed for a while and then discarded as new things replaced the old.

At two years old, Lillie Tabor was featured on the cover of Harper's Bazaar *magazine.* PHOTOGRAPH BY ROSE & COMPANY, COURTESY OF DENVER PUBLIC LIBRARY, SPECIAL COLLECTIONS.

But the extravagant lifestyle the Tabor family enjoyed was about to come crashing down. The question of monetary backing for the U.S. dollar had been a concern in Washington, D.C. In the spring of 1891, Republican President Benjamin Harrison and his wife arrived in Leadville. Tabor greeted him and showed him the fabulous silver mines. Tabor hoped that the president would understand that silver was the natural backing of the nation's currency. But it was not to be. The Populists split the election and Democrat Grover Cleveland was elected president. And the Democrats favored gold. On August 1, 1893, the U.S. Senate voted to repeal the Sherman Silver Purchase Act, which had backed silver over gold.

Overnight Leadville's mines closed and Colorado was plunged into recession. In March 1894, the price of silver reached its bottom at sixty-one cents per ounce. Tabor lost nearly all of his investments. What he didn't lose, he borrowed against to save the rest of his holdings. The Tabors were now desperate. Baby turned to her brother, Peter McCourt, who had become rich, thanks to Tabor, to save the Tabor Opera House. He refused. Their mansion on Sherman Street was foreclosed on. They were losing everything. By some saving grace, Tabor had managed to retain the Matchless silver mine although it was shut down.

The Tabors moved into a small suite at the Windsor Hotel, which Tabor still owned shares in. The city of Denver graciously gave Tabor a job as postmaster of Denver. It was meager pay, but he was glad to have it. In April 1899, Tabor fell ill and was diagnosed with appendicitis. He was too weak to undergo the relatively new medical procedure. Baby stayed by his bedside day and night. When it seemed as if the end was near, Baby summoned a priest from Sacred Heart Church. Tabor was baptized in the Catholic faith and he received the last rites. Finally, on the morning of April 10, Horace Austin Warner Tabor died at the Windsor Hotel in Denver. He was sixty-eight years old. Forty-four-year-old Baby Doe Tabor was now a widow.

Tabor's death was front-page news in most newspapers across the state and even the country. The *Denver Post* headline was "Death of Postmaster H. A. W. Tabor." The stories and obituaries were straightforward. Most were afraid to praise him too highly in light of his personal life. Incredibly, the governor ordered flags flown at half-mast and sent a card of condolence to "Widow Tabor." Soon telegrams arrived and flowers filled the hotel suite.

The ceremony following Tabor's death was astonishing. Tabor's body lay in state under the capitol rotunda in Denver. Later, a parade followed with four bands in the procession. The funeral was held at Sacred Heart Church in Denver, with Father Berry officiating. Baby wore black and was heavily veiled. Following the Catholic service, mourners gathered at the Catholic Calvary block of the City Cemetery for burial. Later, the Colorado State Legislature allocated $600 for a proper tombstone.

Baby and the girls were forced to move from the Windsor Hotel to meager shelter near downtown.[21] Baby spent most of her time trying to find financial backing for what few holdings Tabor had left her, including the Matchless Mine. She let other obligations go unpaid. In early 1901, McGovern Undertaking Parlors filed suit against Baby for nonpayment. The court case made news in all the papers and the State House got involved, introducing a bill to pay for Postmaster Tabor's funeral bill. When Baby heard of this, she went to the state capitol and asked that the bill be withdrawn; she would pay her own bills. A *Denver Herald* reporter wrote, "Of course the lady feels keenly the humiliation that has been placed upon her, by being placed in the position of a mendicant at the public treasury."

More and more stories of Mrs. Tabor's financial woes were appearing in the papers in Denver and in Leadville. When things got really tough, Baby sold some of her jewelry, but she held on to cherished items such as her wedding dress and Tabor's awarded watch fob. It is true that it was a humiliating experience for Baby, but she did the best she could, no matter the hardship. In a rare interview with the *Denver Times,* dated October 7, 1900, Baby Doe Tabor said, "Say if you must say anything, that the property losses are as nothing compared with the loss of my noble husband. Deal gently with him, for the best thing he left the world was his memory, which I love."

It should be mentioned at this juncture in her story that so many writers have claims that Baby Doe Tabor was a "gold digger" and only after Tabor's money. But if that had been the case, she would have ignored this financial obligation, found another rich husband, and lived happily ever after. No, Tabor was her one true love and she carried that love to her grave.

In the summer of 1901, Baby and the girls moved to Leadville and lived in the shaft house at the Matchless Mine. It was her mine now and there would be no rent. However, the girls were a little leery of the idea. Lillie was a grown girl by now and Silver was a lively teenager. While Silver considered the move a bit of an adventure, it was now Lillie who was humiliated. By the end of the summer, she wired Baby's family in Oshkosh for train fare and went to Wisconsin and out of the Tabor life in Colorado. Several years later, Silver Dollar also abandoned her mother. Moving to Chicago, she told her mother she was entering a convent. It was a lie. In 1925, Silver Dollar died. She was found in a flop house, scalded from an overturned kettle of hot water. Silver Dollar Tabor was thirty-six years old.

Baby could often be seen walking to Leadville from her mine in ragged clothing, burlap sacks wrapped around her feet and a wool hat keeping her head warm. She often visited the Delaware Hotel, where the owner, Mr. Callaway, invited her to seat herself at the desk in his office, and she wrote many letters. The grocers and meat butchers always offered their goods to Mrs. Tabor on credit, something she refused to accept. The *Leadville Herald Democrat* had the following story regarding Mrs. Tabor's finances:

> Since the death of her husband, Mrs. Tabor's lines have not fallen in pleasant places. She has, however, pinned her faith on the Matchless mine. Even

> before he died, Mr. Tabor believed that this property would save him from financial embarrassment.
>
> Mr. Tabor sought as a last resort to borrow money on the property, he having in the meantime organized the Tabor Mines and Mills company on the basis of the Matchless mine.
>
> Mrs. Tabor has made earnest efforts to lift this debt. She has made application to a score of prominent mining men and would have probably succeeded in securing assistance but for the fact that no one could see that the Matchless mine was worth anything.

In fact, the 1903 Leadville City Directory contains the following: "MATCHLESS MINE - Fryer Hill; Mrs. H. A. W. Tabor, owner; produced over $3,000,000 in silver and lead from the first contact; main shaft 420 feet; blue lime 200 feet; now producing siliceous iron carrying silver; operated by J. O. Collerette."

For the next thirty-five years, Baby Doe Tabor lived alone in the shaft house at the Matchless Mine, sometimes working the mine herself, and hoping for the day she would see silver ore produced. From time to time she did get financial help, primarily from those who had known and respected her husband. Men like Denver businessman J. K. Mullen, W. S. Stratton of Cripple Creek, and Horace Bennett.

In 1917, George W. Casey, an insurance agent, leased the mine for the war effort. The company, George W. Casey & Associates, supplied nearly twenty-five tons of fluxing iron ore to the Arkansas Valley Smelter. However, the return was so small that the operation was soon discontinued. It was also about this time that the Tabor Opera House in Leadville was sold to the Elk's Club, with a portion of the profit going to Baby Doe Tabor. In 1928, the Shorego Mining Company began foreclosure on the Matchless Mine. In an interview with the *Denver Times,* Mrs. Tabor was quoted as saying:

> The mortgage is held by J. K. Mullen, a Denver multimillionaire, who gladly loaned me $14,000 on the mine in December of 1926. The mortgage was to run for seven years, but I told him to foreclose in order to clear the title of the mine. Rather than have his name connected with the foreclosure against the Tabors, whose very great friend he had been all his life, he organized the Shorego Mining Company, which he is the principal stockholder.

When the foreclosure was completed in 1928, the new owner, the Shorego Mining Company, through the compassion of J. K. Mullen, allowed Mrs. Tabor to remain living in the mining shack. A year later, Peter McCourt died and left his carriage stock to his estranged sister.

In the summer of 1930, work began again on the Matchless Mine. It did not last long, as the following report from the August 27, 1930, issue of the *Herald Democrat* reflects:

> Failure of six men employed at the Matchless mine for the past month to receive their wages led to a stoppage of operations there Saturday night. In the latter part of July the men were employed for the purpose of removing the old and worn out boiler and replacing it with another one from the Doty shaft on Poverty Flats. This operation lasted for a brief time, but when funds gave out, the men started to quit.
>
> Much secrecy was observed regarding the resumption of the operations at the Matchless mine, which has come into the possession of the Shorego mining company [*sic*] Mrs. Tabor, ever hopeful, lives alone at the mine.

Due to the decline in the ore industry following World War I, the Matchless Mine remained inoperable for many years. Baby Doe Tabor lived alone at the mine in despair and loneliness. She was known to chase people off the property with a shotgun.

Baby Doe Tabor stands in front of her cabin home at the Matchless Mine, circa 1930. PHOTOGRAPH BY FLORENCE M. GREENLEAF, COURTESY OF DENVER PUBLIC LIBRARY, SPECIAL COLLECTIONS.

She soon became a pitiful old relic of the past. Baby did not deny she was lonely. In the summer of 1934, she reluctantly accepted the company and eventually the friendship of Naomie Pointers, also known as Sue Bonnie. Sue, much younger than Baby, wandered into Leadville seeking an existence during the trying years of the Great Depression. The companionship of Sue Bonnie was the only connection Baby Doe Tabor had at this point in her life. The two women spent hours retelling their lives and sharing their hopes and dreams with each other. Completely trusting Sue, Baby told her of her purpose for remaining at the Matchless, and somehow, Sue understood.

In early March 1935, a severe winter storm rolled over the mountain range. It was Sue Bonnie's habit, during such storms, to look out her window to see if smoke was coming from the Matchless cabin. One morning Sue saw no smoke. It was too treacherous to climb up to the cabin, so she waited and watched. Finally on the morning of March 7, Sue and a friend, Tom French, made their way through three-foot snowdrifts up to the cabin.

With no response to their knocking on the door, Tom lifted Sue up to peek in the window. There she saw Baby Doe Tabor frozen to the floor, her arms outstretched. Her long thirty-five-year struggle to honor her beloved husband was over. Elizabeth Bonduel McCourt Doe Tabor was dead at the age of eighty-one.

Her funeral was held at Leadville's Church of the Annunciation, the same church where years earlier, Margaret Tobin Brown had married J. J. Brown. The only relative to attend was her younger brother, Willard McCourt. Her daughter Lillie, now married and living in Wisconsin, refused to attend. Burial was at Denver's Catholic cemetery, Mount Olivet. Later, Tabor's casket was removed to be buried beside his beloved wife. Expenses were paid by the Shorego Mining Company, the false company J. K. Mullen had set up to help Mrs. H. A. W. Tabor.

Pallbearers carry the casket of Baby Doe Tabor at her funeral in 1935. PHOTOGRAPH OF DENVER PUBLIC LIBRARY, SPECIAL COLLECTIONS.

Once known as the most beautiful woman in the West, Elizabeth McCourt Doe Tabor, affectionately known as Baby Doe, was the embodiment of a rags to riches story, with an unfortunate twist that left her in rags.

Yet she never lost her pride or her love for her husband and family.

Among Dr. Janet Zaph Briggs' many accomplishments, she was the first woman to earn a mining engineering degree from Stanford University. PHOTOGRAPH FROM THE 1931 STANFORD QUAD YEARBOOK, COURTESY OF STANFORD UNIVERSITY.

Janet Zaph Briggs: Mining Engineer

When Baby Doe Tabor died, Leadville was in the midst of the Great Depression. Because of the bad economy, metal ores were nearly worthless. But those unbelievable holes in the ground refused to quit and new discoveries were just out of reach. However, one woman discovered a breakthrough technology to uncover and process those ores, just when it was needed the most.

Janet Zaph Briggs was at the forefront of twentieth century mining technology. She advanced a theory in the experimental metallurgy of iron. Born February 7, 1912, in Santa Ana, California, Dr. Briggs received her doctorate in metallurgical theory at Stanford University in California. She was the first woman to achieve such a feat. She would complete her doctoral studies at the University of Leoben in Austria. In 1933, she arrived in Leadville to test her theory at the Climax Mine.

There had been some talk, rumors mostly, of an undeniable ore at the mine up on Bartlett Mountain, just north of town. Nobody paid much attention until Dr. Briggs came to town.

In 1879, Charles Senter had filed a few claims on Bartlett Mountain, near Fremont Pass, about twelve miles northeast of Leadville. The mountain got its name from the uphill grade of the Denver & South Park Railroad track. Senter's mineral samples, white rock with black streaks, were eventually determined to be sulfide of molybdenum. It was a funny name that no one knew how to pronounce, and no one knew how to use the new ore, so the mining claims sat for more than thirty years. Few people paid attention to the mine or the ore. A newspaper article now and then, such as this one from the *Leadville Herald Democrat* of September 4, 1911, reminded people that "at present the metal is found very sparsely scattered in the ores and the problem involved in handling the ores is to discover a process by which the molybdenum compounds can be concentrated so that they may be smeltered at a profit. In the past the molybdenum found in the district has been neglected owing to the cost of having it treated."

By World War I, molybdenum was being used to strengthen steel, and Senter provided it. But it was difficult to mine. It was during this time that Senter sold out to an investment group that organized the Climax Molybdenum Company, retaining a twenty-five percent share in the company. In mid-December, a group of statewide mining capitalists toured the mine at Climax. The *Herald Democrat* reported:

> The visit to Climax of a distinguished party of mining men and financiers, including Spencer Penrose, Thomas McNeil, A. E. Carlton, the president of the Colorado Midland, and B. H. Hopkins, the head of one of the largest molybdenum producing companies of Canada, is significant of other and even more important developments in that section. The party visited the Climax area under the guidance of Mr. O. A. King, general manager of the Pingrey Mines and Ore reduction Company which has large holdings in the region.

By February 1918, the mining property boasted a mill, a crusher, bunkhouses, and a mile-long tramway that brought 300 miners to work each day. By the end of the year the mine grew to become the world's largest underground mine.

Shortly after the end of World War I, however, the miners went on strike. Their pay had been reduced by a dollar an hour due to low demand for the ore. After three days, the miners agreed to a fifty-cent-an-hour wage reduction. It mattered little as the mine shut down at the end of 1919.

Dr. Janet Zaph Briggs arrived at Climax to put her smelting theory to the test. Her research led to the successful smelting of iron and the direct production of forgable steel from ore in the smelting pits.

So successful was her theory, she was awarded the title of "Engineer," an honor Dr. Briggs carried throughout her career at Climax Molybdenum Mine in Leadville. In no large part due to Dr. Briggs and her discoveries, molybdenum was in high demand during World War II, thus saving Leadville's economy during these trying times.

During World War II Dr. Briggs' smelting process was a such a huge success that Dr. Briggs received a patent in 1945 for the process of making hardened steel. By the end of the decade, Climax Molybdenum Company controlled eighty-six percent of the world's production. By 1953 the company had built a hospital, a school, and a grocery store for the miners and their families.

Because of the company's success, due in no small part to Dr. Briggs and her work, she was made vice president and continued in that role until 1970. However, even in retirement, Dr. Briggs continued her work in metallurgy. She moved to New York City to be closer to the international community. She was very familiar with the international stage and spoke Chinese, Japanese, Swedish, Spanish, Romanian, and Ukranian. In 1971, Dr. Briggs was given the Award of Excellence by the North American Precis Syndicate (an information outreach service company).

While on a business trip to Tokyo in 1974, Dr. Briggs received the Fourth Class of Order of the Sacred Treasure by the emperor of Japan, "in recognition of her contribution to the development of Japan's steel industry." Unfortunately, shortly after receiving the honor, while still in Japan, Dr. Janet Briggs died of a heart attack. She was sixty-one years old.

In 1989, Dr. Janet Zaph Briggs was inducted into the National Mining Hall of Fame in Leadville.

Notes

1. Augusta Tabor files. Western History Department, Denver Public Library.
2. ibid.
3. ibid.
4. ibid.
5. ibid.
6. ibid.
7. ibid.
8. ibid.
9. ibid.
10. ibid.

11. Today, the United Bank building occupies this site.
12. Augusta Tabor Scrapbooks, Denver Public Library.
13. Blair, Edward, *Leadville: Colorado's Magic City.* Fred Pruett Books, 1995. p. 177.
14. Taped interviews conducted by her lawyer, Fred Mazzula, held at History Center Colorado.
15. ibid.
16. Taped interviews conducted by her lawyer, Fred Mazzula, held at History Center Colorado.
17. *The Herald Democrat,* "The Woman of Leadville," p. 6.
18. Taped interviews conducted by her lawyer, Fred Mazzula, held at History Center Colorado.
19. Lake County Public Library, Colorado Mountain History Collection.
20. Most writers of Baby Doe's story repeat this event as having occurred at the Saddle Rock Cafe, a Caroline Bancroft concoction. The Saddle Rock Cafe did not open until 1881. See Lake County Public Library, Colorado Mountain History Collection.
21. It should be noted that, among her many treasures, Baby Doe Tabor's wedding dress and Horace Tabor's watch fob are occasionally on display at the Colorado History Center in Denver.

4

THE WOMEN OF LUDLOW

To the woman of American birth fellowship with the American people is a powerful offset to isolation, even though she may live in the remotest of coal-mining communities. This is not the case with the woman belonging to the family of the foreign-born worker. To her the coal-mining community—whether populous independent town or isolated company controlled mining camp—is America.

—U.S. Women's Bureau, 1915

ABOUT 70 MILLION YEARS AGO, the Rocky Mountains were still rising out of the sea and coastal swamps covered much of present-day southern Colorado. Ferns, horsetails, and other plants grew, reproduced, died, and rotted, adding inches and then layers of peat to the swamp floor until, after a few million years, the peat in some places was hundreds of feet deep. That peat was buried under sediment, and then for another million years it was dried, squeezed, and cooked underground. It became dense, hard, and dark in color. It was flammable. Geologists called it coal, and it was a valuable fuel for everything from heating homes and businesses to powering ships and railroad locomotives. Coal was also an important ingredient in the process of making steel. In the 1800s, it was quickly recognized as one of Colorado's most valuable natural resources.

The state's coal outcroppings occurred on the Western Slope and in great abundance in parts of southern Colorado, including east of the Continental Divide in the region around the town of Trinidad. Men came from far and wide—even from as far away as Ireland, Wales, and Eastern Europe—to toil in Colorado's coal mines, but the work was physically demanding and dangerous, often for meager pay. Unlike gold and silver mining, the men who worked in the coalfields had no hope of "striking it rich." Their primary ambition was to earn a livable wage while avoiding death from explosion, fire, tunnel collapse, or toxic gases. But life in a coal camp or company town often seemed stacked against the miners.

The Ludlow Massacre

John D. Rockefeller 's Colorado Fuel and Iron Company (CF&I) operated a number of coal mines in southern Colorado, along with a steel mill in Pueblo. Mine workers lived in isolated company towns or camps, and miners and their families were forced to buy food and other essentials from company stores. The ratio of prices to wages was such that miners were usually in debt to the very company that employed them. Coal miners' wives learned to economize and be thrifty. Angela Tonso remembered:

> We used to buy ranch butter, you know, we bought it for 15 cents a pound. And we used to get a pail of lard. The butter we used sparsely for the toast, sometimes not even that because [we had only] one pound a month for the whole family. But we used to use the lard instead, you know. And when we fry something, you know, we saved that, especially a pork chop. Oh my God, that was a luxury then. And we saved that grease, you know, pork chop grease to use it and use it.[1]

Indeed, the women learned to conserve, improvise, and make the best of nature's resources. Josephine Bazanelle, a miner's wife, recalled, "They used to scrub by hand, go fetch the water a mile or two [at] 3:00 in the morning. We used to make salami out of jackrabbit meat, believe it or not."[2]

Company control of the miners and their wives also extended to the children. They grew up fast in the mining camps; as soon as they were physically able, they were given household chores. For the boys twelve years old and up, they worked in the mines alongside their fathers. Girls of the same age were often encouraged to marry. Before work or marriage, the children attended some form of schooling. However, at the Ludlow area camps, the schooling included a type of indoctrination of the mostly immigrant children of Rockefeller's employees. Rockefeller hired Dr. Richard Corwin, a medical sociologist, to head up the education process at his CF&I coal camps. Dr. Corwin wrote:

> It is difficult to change the way and manners of adults; their habits have been formed and are not easily altered. With age comes indifference, a desire to be

> left alone and a loss of ambition; but not so is it with the young. Children are tractable, easily managed and molded, have no set ways to correct and recast; hence the importance of kindergarten.[3]

All teachers were hired by CF&I and expected to follow Dr. Corwin's guidelines. One miner and father, Clarence Cordova, later recalled, "You know who had the say so about the teachers? It's the supers. The supers used to hire the teachers. They used to pick out the teachers. If they didn't like a teacher, she wouldn't be there long. They would fire her and get someone else."[4]

The coal miners and their families were a diverse group. They were immigrants from several different countries, bringing their cultures with them. They worked alongside white Americans, African Americans, and Hispanic Americans whose ancestors had been in America for generations. At Ludlow, the workforce of about 1,200 men was composed of more than 100 ethnicities, but the majority were Polish, Italian, Welsh, Russian, and Greek. Company officials deemed these multi-ethnic workers to be lower-class people and blamed them for the divisiveness between labor and management.

Over the years a few laws were enacted to ensure safety for the miners. But in Colorado, Rockefeller's CF&I ignored the existing laws, resulting in one of the highest death rates among miners in the country. Miners endured other labor hardships. Ludlow miners were paid by the ton of the coal they extracted and received no pay for "dead work" such as blasting tunnels, shoring up mine walls and ceilings, and laying rail track for transporting the coal. The workday began before sunrise and ended after sundown. Very often, young sons worked underground alongside their fathers.

In the summer of 1913, the United Mine Workers began organizing the coal miners, over 11,000 strong, employed at CF&I. John Lawson, an executive board member of District 15 who started working in Colorado mines in 1895, directed the strike action in the Trinidad area through an office there. Mike Livoda, who spoke four languages, and Louis Tikas, who grew up in Crete and had worked as an interpreter for the union, were among the organizers.

In August 1913, the union leaders invited CF&I representatives to meet and discuss the miners' grievances: low pay, the enforcement of safety regulations, long hours, and management control, among others. Their list of demands was simple—enforcement of an eight-hour workday, a ten percent pay raise, and the option to live and trade outside of the company-owned boundaries. Rockefeller refused. The miners refused to back down.

In early September, labor activist Mary Harris "Mother" Jones came from West Virginia to assist with preparing the miners for a potential walkout. Mother Jones was a militant crusader for the rights of laboring men and women, as well as an idolized de facto leader of the United Mine Workers of America. A fiery speaker, she was often used by the union to encourage miners to stay on strike and to organize protest marches. As such, she was one of the nationally known participants in the Colorado strike.

Top CF&I officials continued to disregard the miners' demands. Within a month's time the miners went on strike. Union leaders provided a small stipend for the striking miners. Twice a month each miner received $2.50 and an additional thirty-five cents for each child.

Because the striking miners refused to back down, Rockefeller made his next move. He evicted the miners and their families from their homes, which were mere shacks. In turn, the United Mine Workers provided land and tents not far from the mines for the miners and their families to live in while the strike went on. The largest camp was Ludlow, about twelve miles northwest of Trinidad on a windswept prairie where two canyons emptied out of the foothills. In retaliation, Rockefeller ordered his men to hire a detective agency to protect the company's interests. In actuality, the Baldwin-Felts Detective Agency men were hired guns expected to intimidate the miners and end the strike.

Among the wealthiest men in America, John D. Rockefeller Sr. and Jr., shown here in 1915, were both reviled by many miners and other laborers. PHOTOGRAPH COURTESY OF THE LIBRARY OF CONGRESS, LC-USZ62-48511.

The Ludlow tent colony was located on vacant land near the entrances of the two canyons leading to the mines and the small community of Ludlow,

Colorado. Just to the east was the Colorado and Southern Railway line. An elevated wood water tank of the railroad lay on the west side of the tracks.[5] Mary Thomas, a fiery redhead, was a native of Wales and a miner's wife at Ludlow. She later published a memoir and recalled the surrounding countryside:

> What a bleak view. For miles and miles there was an uneven prairie, with small hills scattered all about. Half a mile in back [north] of the colony was the deep arroyo which took the waters from the melting snow to the valley below. Ludlow was at the foot of the narrow canyon that climbed the steep hills to the many mining camps.[6]

Notations on photographs of the Ludlow tent colony taken during early 1914, and a map of the colony prepared by the Colorado National Guard in May 1914, indicate that there were six east-west streets. Front Street lay closest to the county road on the south, with 2nd, 3rd, 4th, 5th, and 6th Streets following from south to north. Main Street was the only north-south street. Approximately two-thirds of the tents were located east of the main street and one-third to the west.[7] Mary Thomas noted, "The tents were arranged in rows following a west-southwest to east-northeast alignment. Each of the tents was numbered on numerically designated streets so we could be located quickly."

Near the center of the camp, a public square included a raised platform where formal gatherings and meetings were held. A large bell next to the platform was used to signal emergencies and a bulletin board contained updated posts regarding union reports on strike developments. Next to the platform was a large multi-use tent that was used as a school as well as for community purposes such as dances, religious services, and meetings. Mary Thomas remembered, "The circus-like tent featured a big pot-bellied stove in the center which nearly broiled the people close to it. Both the platform and the community tent proudly displayed American flags, raised and lowered each day with solemn ceremony."

The UMWA headquarters tent was located along Front Street at the south edge of the camp, as were the dispensary and offices of Doctors Harvey and Davis. The camp store was situated near the southwest corner of the camp. Camp infrastructure included a trash dump, privies, sanitary ditches, and cellars for storage and shelter. Wagons brought water to the tent colony in barrels. The union provided heavy Excelsior stoves from Quincy, Illinois, for each tent, and contemporary photographs of the camp show stovepipes projecting through the roofs. Coal provided to the striking miners for cooking and heating was in short supply, and the women learned to prioritize it for cooking rather than heating. Clotheslines were put up west of the tents (between the colony and the railroad tracks) to facilitate laundry chores. Hygiene was another matter. Trenches were dug around the colony for outhouses. During the freezing winter months, however, the miners and their families used chamber pots inside their tents. The camp trash dump was in the northwest corner of the tract on the south bank of Del Agua Arroyo.

The tents erected for the miners and their families were made of canvas and had gabled roofs. They were erected by first digging a shallow basin, then laying wooden joists directly on the ground to support a wooden platform and frame. The tents were

Women and children stand in front of a tent home in the Ludlow Colony, 1913. PHOTOGRAPH COURTESY OF DENVER PUBLIC LIBRARY, SPECIAL COLLECTIONS.

placed along the ridge lines from north-northwest to south-southeast. Most of the tents had center entrances on the south side. Many tent entrances had a wooden floorboard and some even had wooden doors. Some of the tents featured raised wood floors and short wood sidewalls. Most of the tents were sixteen by eighteen feet. Some families had double tents, using one room for a kitchen and children's sleeping area, and the other for the parent's bedroom.[8] Families living in the camp excavated beneath their tents to create areas for storage and for safety in the event of an attack. The tent cellars were also intended as a place of security for women and children as well as a center for peaceful household activities. Pregnant women gave birth in the cellars rather than aboveground in a tent. Children often slept in the cellars that served as bedrooms, and their parents instructed them to hide in the cellars if the colony were under attack.

The mining families brought all of their furniture and other worldly possessions to the tent colony. Mary Thomas recounted, "Many families put old linoleums on the floor to cover cracks and keep out drafts." Apparently Mary liked the idea, as she did the same, purchasing

> two bright linoleums for our tent with its twin cots. The store gave me three empty wooden orange crates with dividers in them which, when put on end, made fine stands with a shelf underneath for food or dishes. I covered them with the tablecloths I [had] been given for a wedding present. I put my bright bedspreads on the cots, and curtains to match which I hung over the two small windows. These, too, I had brought from Wales. I got three chairs from the commissary to round out our furnishings, and took great pride in hanging my trinkets on the four-foot high side walls.[9]

Mary Hannah Thomas later wrote a memoir that included her firsthand account of the events at Ludlow. A native of Ogmore Valley in South Wales, Mary met and married a Welsh miner at a young age. The couple had two children, Olga and Rachael, before the husband deserted his family for America. Undaunted, in time, Mary set out to find him. With two toddlers in tow, Mary Thomas, at twenty-four years old, set sail for America in 1913. Mary happened to arrive in Colorado at the same time that the United Mine Workers of America was organizing in the coalfields there. Mary was recruited to help sign up the miners, primarily for her singing talent. Mary settled in at Ludlow and made a home for herself and her girls. Ironically enough, Mary soon found her husband, who was also at Ludlow. The couple reconciled for a time but it was not to last.[10]

Ludlow was the largest of the union tent colonies established during the 1913–1914 Colorado coal strike. The number of tents varied over time with increases and decreases in the settlement's population. As the strike continued, some miners departed to seek work elsewhere and the population of the tent colony declined. For example, on the second day of the strike, the *Denver Express* reported that there were 16 tents present. The tent count jumped to 100 by September 27 and to 200 by September 30, when the *Denver Express* called the camp "a white city of a thousand souls." Mary Thomas put the camp population at 1,200 and close to 150 tents.[11]

The winter of 1913–1914 was particularly severe. Snow came early—the October 10, 1913, *Denver Express* reported, "The snow has brought intense suffering to the miners, wives and children housed in the light tents of the colony." High winds accompanied record-breaking snowfall, with thirty to fifty inches of snow piling up from Cheyenne, Wyoming, south through Trinidad. The tents at Ludlow were just barely adequate. Mary Thomas recalled:

> Many mornings my children and I would wake up to see tents about to collapse from the weight of the snow. They looked like igloos. It was terrible weather at that time. But we determined to stick together there because we had put up with such a lot and believed we would rather suffer anything than go back to work under the conditions that they had been working.[12]

During the winter of 1913–1914, heavy snows added work and stress to life in the Ludlow Colony. *PHOTOGRAPH COURTESY OF DENVER PUBLIC LIBRARY, SPECIAL COLLECTIONS.*

Many residents formed a group and monitored conditions around the clock, scraping paths and clearing away snow to prevent the tents from caving in. Historic photographs show huge banks of snow piled throughout the colony. Caroline Tomsic later recalled, "It's the closeness of the people, closeness of the miners. And something about camp life, after you moved out you miss what you had there, because people were so close."[13]

Then, just a week later on October 17, 1913, an armor-plated car (soon dubbed the "Death Special") drove through the tent colony at Forbes, Colorado, firing bullets at the tents and killing one person. They were known to be Rockefeller's hired guns. As a result, the striking miners at Ludlow and elsewhere decided to arm themselves.

Rockefeller's hired guns, under the auspices of the Baldwin-Felts Detective Agency, began raiding the Ludlow tent colony on a regular basis using Gatling guns and high-power rifles. Militia rifle and machine gun fire claimed the lives of at least five strikers plus an eleven-year-old boy and an eighteen-year-old passerby. The unexpected attack was the fateful climax of miners attempting to achieve freedom from oppression at the hands of coal company officials. More than 300 Baldwin-Felts agents were quickly named sheriff's deputies by local law enforcement. The union responded by having its organizers commissioned as game wardens, so that they, too, would be armed if the government suspended the right of ordinary citizens to carry guns.

Rockefeller demanded that Governor Elias M. Ammons bring in the Colorado National Guard. Finally, an agreement was made by the two men. Ammons agreed to call up the militia and dispatch them to Ludlow, and Rockefeller agreed to pay their salary for the duration of time it took to squelch the strikers. When the soldiers arrived, the miners actually welcomed them, thinking they were there to keep law and order. They couldn't have been more wrong. One of the miners' wives, Pearl Jolly, later wrote, "We didn't want trouble. The militia came and we welcomed them. We got two brass bands for them. We danced with them and they had their meals with us but soon things began to change."

Indeed, at first the miners thought the Guard was sent to protect them. They greeted their arrival with flags and cheers. Then the miners soon realized the Guard was sent by the governor and Rockefeller to break the strike. The Guard brought in strikebreakers under the cover of night, not telling them there was a strike. Guardsmen beat miners, arrested them by the hundreds, and patrolled the tent city constantly, raiding, threatening, and even shooting their guns on occasion.

The striking miners prepared to defend themselves. A map produced by the Colorado National Guard and other sources showed rifle pits in several locations, including the northwest and northeast corners of the tent area and along the south bank of Del Agua Arroyo to the north.[14] Angela Tonso told of being on the front lines and smuggling guns to the miners: "We put the rifle under our coat there and half in the boots and half under the arm," she said, "and have our [other] arm free so the militia they see that we ain't got nothing."[15]

The miners' wives were more than willing to aid their husbands. This was their fight as well. They were courageous in defending their families, their homes, and their way of life. And Mother Jones cheered them on:

> It is not the demonstration or violence or the speeches that will win the strike, if it is won, but the simple continuity of feeding and washing and cleaning that goes on between those canvas walls, those trips along the muddy paths between the wash lines and the coal piles and the store. And if the women give up one day on the scrimping and hoarding and patching and say they've had enough, then the strike is lost.[16]

Mary Thomas noted that most of the adults in the tent colony were under thirty years of age and most of the children were less than six years old. The large number of children ensured that women fulfilled many traditional gender-specific roles at Ludlow, including child care, food preparation, tent decoration and cleaning, and laundry tasks. However, these women (and sometimes children) also fulfilled important roles in the strike actions that demonstrated their significance to the labor movement. Caroline Tomsic remembered the important part women played: "Just as big as the men, the women big, play a big role what I mean. And tried to the best we could, you know."

Women gathered along the dirt road south of the colony and along the fence near the railroad tracks to the west to express welcome or voice outrage at the arrival and activities of troops, company guards, and strikebreakers. They greeted members of the public and government officials who visited the camp and often submitted to newspaper interviews. Pearl Jolly, one of the wives, later told the Commission of Industrial Relations that the militiamen and Pinkerton men kept their guns trained on the women and children in the camp.[17]

The miners refused to submit to the National Guard, the governor, or Rockefeller's goons. Someone decided that tougher measures were needed to end the strike. Whether it was Rockefeller himself or General John Chase, who was in command of the Colorado National Guard, an order was given to attack the Ludlow

Given the events that were about to unfold, this photograph taken the morning of April 20, 1914, shows a remarkably quiet scene at the Ludlow Colony. PHOTOGRAPH COURTESY OF DENVER PUBLIC LIBRARY, SPECIAL COLLECTIONS.

tent colony. Patrick Hamrock, commander of the National Guard, ordered his men to place a machine gun above the colony.

No one knows who fired the first shot. Witnesses remembered seeing two National Guard companies in the hills watching the tent city below. Other witnesses remembered hearing a loud explosion. Then all hell broke loose.

At 9:55 A.M. on April 20, 1914, a loud explosion shocked the strikers and their wives and children. It seemed that a bomb had gone off at the tent of Major Hamrock, apparently as a signal to the militiamen surrounding the camp on all sides that it was time to open fire on miners and the tent colony. Mary Thomas later stated that the first indication of the fight that was to come was when she heard the sound of a bomb and she saw people run out of their tents. She recalled:

> Tikas instructed women and children to flee for their lives and men to grab their rifles and run to the hills. Suddenly the prairie was covered with human beings running in all directions like ants. No one had time to get anything, save to pick up whatever food was on the table. We all ran as we were, some with babies on their backs, in whatever clothes we were wearing, leaving our tent homes behind us, snatching what we could take with us immediately, not even thinking through the clouds of panic. We were terrified.[18]

Women quickly organized to protect their families and help the men. By their continued presence in a location where violence was erupting everywhere, these women demonstrated their commitment to the striking miners. When the attack came, some women sought safety with their children in places such as the cellars dug under their tents, while others continued to assist the men on the front lines.

There were not more than forty rifles in the tent colony. The rest of the men scattered to the hills in a vain effort to draw the militiamen's fire away from the tent colony and their families. At 10 A.M. a second bomb exploded. Ten seconds later, a third shot was fired and the slaughter of Ludlow began. Helen Korich, a seven-year-old Croatian girl, recalled:

> The next day [after Easter Sunday] the shooting started. I had my white lace dress on, my Easter dress. The weather was beautiful. They started shooting their machine guns at us, and they knew people were in the basements [cellars]. My dad got his gun out when they started shooting at us. I wanted to go with my dad. But he said, 'No, you can not go with me. Go home, go with Mama.' We were out of the tent, and my sister came after me and pulled me back by my hair. I was so mad! I thought they would kill him. The shells were going right by my ear. We knew they were going to murder all of us. They were shooting all over, and the union men were scattered. We walked down under a bridge where two union men were shooting. One got shot and fell, and I stepped on him. I was so scared I ran straight through some barbed wire and it tore my Easter dress, but I just kept running, pulling that barbed wire and lace, for what seemed like miles and miles.[19]

Helen, her two sisters, and her mother holding a baby boy all ran as fast as they could to get away from the flying bullets. Helen later told reporters about the family's two dogs, saying, "They shot her [the dog]. They killed the puppy, too. I remember how quiet everything was. You could hear all the shooting, but nobody yelled. They were going to kill us all."[20]

When union leader John Lawson heard about the attack, he gathered men and supplies and headed toward Ludlow, but his party was unable to reach the colony site due to continued gunfire. It is believed that it was Lawson who told Louis Tikas to hold out until relief got there. Then Lawson headed out in the direction of the tent colony through the arroyo, where he found miners lined up and others lying in rifle pits.

The leader of the striking miners, Louis Tikas, spent the first half of the day dodging bullets and machine gun fire, often in a cross-fire, trying to rescue women and children and taking them to places of safety. Pearl Jolly, a leader of the women of the tent colony, later testified that Tikas worked with her during much of the day to get the women and children out of danger. As the strikers' position grew more desperate, however, Tikas ordered the miners to retreat to the hills northeast of camp. When Tikas finally realized the futility of his actions, he called Major Hamrock in an effort to negotiate a truce. Tikas then met with Hamrock but his plea for a ceasefire was refused, and Major Hamrock ordered a detachment of troops to take up a position on Water Tank Hill. This was a strategic elevation south of the Ludlow train depot, about three-quarters of a mile south of the tent colony. Back in the tent camp, a group of strikers disturbed by the soldiers' presence on the hill congregated around Tikas and argued in favor of armed resistance to any further attempt by Guardsmen to enter and search the colony. It was for naught. Tikas never returned from his meeting with Hamrock. He was taken prisoner, although some of the gunmen wanted to hang the Greek leader. Lieutenant Karl E. "Monty" Linderfelt then hit Tikas on the head, crushing his skull and killing him instantly. Realizing what he did, Linderfelt then shot him in the back, making it look like Tikas was killed when he tried to escape.

Soon the first National Guard troops arrived on Water Tank Hill. Major Hamrock, who viewed the movements of the armed strikers as ominous, directed his troops to take battle positions on the hill. Three women, who had been at the depot and saw the troops occupying the position, returned to the tent colony and informed the striking miners of this development.

Viewing the National Guard movements as a threat, some thirty-five to fifty armed Greek strikers began moving from the tent colony to a position in the Colorado & Southeastern Railway bed to the southeast. Other groups within the camp started moving northwest toward Del Agua Arroyo and the Colorado and Southern Railway bridge. The railroad tracks near the colony site would play an important role later in the day. Then Hamrock ordered the detonation of two dynamite bombs to signal other troops in the area of imminent combat. The explosions were interpreted by the strikers as a Guard attack on one of their positions, and a general exchange of gunfire between the National Guard and the strikers began.[21]

Without food, without water, and amid a shower of bullets that pierced their places of shelter, the women and children of Ludlow spent that day running for their lives and hiding in cellars. By this time, the militia knew there were no armed miners there to return their fusillade of bullets. They knew that in those places there were only women and children, and so they wielded the machine guns like fire hoses, cutting down everything in their view as they swerved from one end of the colony to the other and back again.

Women, driven by sheer fear, ran for their lives into the tents and down into the cellars that had been dug for their safety, carrying their babies and herding their young children with them, all while bullets were flying near, above, and all around. At some point, eleven-year-old Frankie Snyder crawled out from under the Snyder family tent to get water for his mother and little sisters, who had become ill from fright. He was shot through the head and killed instantly. His father later asked soldiers who were clearing the area to help him carry his dead son's body out of the rubble. The soldiers refused.

Pearl Jolly, who is often referred to as the "heroine" of the Ludlow Massacre, was trying to help the women and children. She later recalled:

> Mrs. Snyder had six children, and none of them had anything to eat. At 5 o'clock the firing ceased, so she came up out of the cave and brought the children. She had two tents, a kitchen and bedroom. She threw the children in the last corner and set them all in a bunch till it would be possible for her to get something for them to eat. She had been there about two minutes when the oldest boy, 12 years old, had run when the top of his head was blown off, and his brains were spattered over.[22]

Pearl Jolly further testified:

> When the soldiers kept continually shooting into the camp the women asked me to put a white dress on with red crosses, in the hope the soldiers would recognize the universal sign and it would be protection. The soldiers could not help but see it. When I got out there they took it for to be a good target and shot at me as hard as they could.[23]

Nevertheless, Mrs. Jolly soldiered on. During the battle she darted here and there throughout the tent colony, rescuing women and children and aiding the sick and wounded. Although she wore the Red Cross insignia on her arm, the uniformed gunmen tried to kill her, one bullet tearing off the heel of her shoe.

Like Tikas, James Fyler, secretary of the Ludlow union, was another striker who was murdered while a prisoner of the Hamrock-Linderfelt militiamen. Fyler was one of the heroes of that day. With his life in danger, he nevertheless managed to remain on the telephone, giving a reporter the only news of the horror as it occurred in real time. A militiaman shot Fyler at close range with a shotgun, which blew off the front of his face.

Another hero that day was Charles Costa. When the militia began their murderous assault, Costa, along with others in the tent colony who had guns, ran to the hills to return fire, doing all they could to save the women and children, and their homes.

Costa was one of the five men of Ludlow Colony who would pay the penalty of death for fighting for his constitutional rights before the day was over. Costa was shot through the head. As he lay in view of his tented home where women and children were being murdered and incinerated, he asked one of his comrades to sing "Union Forever." A few of the striking miners crowded around him and sang the song as bullets flew around them. And at the same time, in the tent colony below, Costa's wife and three children lay dead. Charles Costa would soon join them.

As morning turned to afternoon, the machine gun fire only intensified, indiscriminately raining down on the tent colony. The Guardsmen later testified that they were justified in their actions, believing that no women and children were still present in the camp. This assertion was contradicted by the survivors, who experienced gunshot wounds and witnessed people being shot and killed. With such gunfire it was nearly impossible for the women and children present to have escaped or been evacuated from the site. If Guardsmen did not see women and children, it was only because the women and children had climbed into the cellars beneath the tents in search of safety from the flying bullets. Historian George McGovern wrote, "It was due to these dugouts [under the tents] and not the humanitarianism of the militia which saved the union families from possible annihilation, for the colony was mercilessly raked by rifle and machine gun fire during the day."[24]

Union members tried to contact the Trinidad UMWA office to request reinforcements and ammunition, but communication lines soon failed. As the battle continued into late afternoon, the Ludlow strikers began to run low on ammunition, giving the soldiers the opportunity to advance northward along the Colorado and Southern Railway tracks from the Ludlow depot under the cover of machine gun fire. At dusk, the arrival of reinforcements, dispatched by the Las Animas County sheriff from Trinidad, assisted the Guardsmen, who finally drove strikers from their positions in Del Agua Arroyo and captured the C&S steel bridge northwest of the colony.

A Colorado and Southern southbound train pulled into Ludlow about 7:20 P.M. A brakeman and a conductor on the train later testified that they saw soldiers firing into the tent colony and also saw one of the Guardsmen rushing the tent area with a flaming torch. Nevertheless, the train slowed as it came between the line of sight of the troops and the strikers, and some of the women and children who had been in the dry well, the pump house, and tent cellars began struggling toward the safety of the train.

Both sides disputed how the fire that caused the destruction of the colony began. Major Hamrock asserted it started spontaneously while his troops were still some distance from the tents. John Lawson initially believed the National Guard used explosive bullets that caused the fire. Some witnesses testified they saw one of the troops setting fire to tents with a broom soaked in coal oil, while others believed that gunfire caused a spark that ignited some ammunition. A military investigating commission later concluded, regardless of how the fire started, the troops spread the blaze: "Beyond a doubt it was seen to intentionally that the fire should destroy the whole of the colony," the commission wrote.[25]

Guardsmen later testified that, as they watched the conflagration spread through the tent colony, they had assumed the camp was abandoned. Lieutenant Karl Linderfelt recalled hearing "the most awful wail, alerting the troops to the fact that women and children were still on the scene."[26]

Women ran into the open, some with their clothing on fire and babies in their arms. Firing ceased, and some officers and soldiers began helping the women and children reach safety. Others looted the strikers' tents, torching and otherwise destroying what they could not take with them. The National Guard investigative panel later concluded that the soldiers ceased to be an army and had become a mob.

In tent No. 1 at the southwest corner of the colony, Mary Petrucci and her three children remained in their underground shelter. When the tent above caught fire, the family ran to the one behind it, where they climbed in a cellar with eleven others already inside.[27] The *New York Times* issue of April 22, 1914, famously described the scene as the tents blazed: "Some [women], braver than the rest, ran into the open and dashed aimlessly among the two hundred tents, which by that time, had become so many torches which swirled their fire and sparks and lighted the scene with ghastly brilliancy."

Several witnesses later testified that the soldiers took oil cans to extend the fire and make it complete without concern for any of the colonists.[28] Margaret Dominiske later testified that she saw "five militiamen cross from the tents that was burning over to those that was not burning, and three of them had torches and two had cans. I don't know what was in the cans, but I think it was oil."[29]

Mrs. Petrucci's husband later recalled, "I was in the hills with the other men. We had our rifles. We saw the flames in the colony. My wife and my children were down there. I could do nothing."[30]

Later that evening, some thirty women and children managed to escape and run to the nearby Powell Ranch. Mrs. Pearl Jolly, along with other women and children, also escaped, making it to a farmhouse late that afternoon.

Thirteen colonists who tried to flee were shot and killed as the tent camp burned to the ground. Mary Thomas was wounded by gunfire as she escaped. She and other women and children made their way to the depot where a freight train stopped just between the Guardsmen and the fleeing colonists. The entire party managed to get on the train and away to safety.

Dawn the next morning presented a scene of utter horror. The Ludlow tent colony lay in smoldering ruin. Metal objects, such as cast-iron stoves and stovepipes, bed frames, and washtubs stood out in the otherwise flattened land of blackened debris. Those items along with bits of broken pottery and glass identified the former locations of tents in the colony. The morning seemed to progress with more and more horrific findings. A telephone lineman discovered the most shocking tragedy of the events thus far, leading the news media to label the event the "Ludlow Massacre."

As the telephone repairman was sifting through the ruins of the disintegrated tent colony, he lifted an iron cot, which was covering a pit under one of the tents. Peering down below, the man saw several charred bodies. The authorities recovered eleven children and four women. Mary Petrucci and Alcarita Pedregone were in the pit but somehow managed to survive, but both lost their children, who suffocated to death. Some years later, Mrs. Petrucci recalled: "I came out of the hole. There was light and lots of smoke. I wandered among the ashes until a priest found me. I couldn't feel anything. I was cold."

A reporter for the *Denver Express* was present when the bodies were removed from the underground pit. He described it as "a perpendicular shaft 10 feet deep, with rude steps carved in the earth sides, and at the bottom a room six feet square and three feet high, hollowed out. The stairs have a concrete rim at the top around the rectangular opening, which has a hinged metal door with strap braces and a metal handle."[31]

The location of the "death pit," as it came to be referred to, was below tent No. 58, in the southwest corner of the tent colony. Later, a coroner's jury found that the victims in the tent cellar died of asphyxiation or fire or both. The thirteen were identified as Cedilena Costa (27) and her children, Lucy Costa (4) and Onafrio Costa (6); Patria Valdez (37) and her children Rudolph Valdez (9), Eulala Valdez (8), Mary Valdez (7), and Elvira Valdez (3 months); the children of Mary Petrucci, Joseph Petrucci (4), Lucy Petrucci (2), and Frank Petrucci (6 months); and the children of Alcarita Pedregone, Rodgerlo Pedregone (6) and Cloriva Pedregone (4).

Linda Linville, the granddaughter of Charles Costa, related what she had been told of the horror her family suffered:

> Charlie was killed at age 31, shot in the head, he was one of the men running away from the colony, hoping to draw fire away from the women and children. On that same day, Cedilena was killed in the cellar beneath the tent. She was 27. The death of an unnamed infant has gone unacknowledged. There is no death certificate, not even a mention in the cemetery record book. The infant was buried in the coffin with Cedilena. . . . The next time my grandmother saw Cedilena, Charlie and the children was in the Trinidad mortuary, where they had to identify the bodies. The official cause of death was listed as asphyxiation, but there is nothing in the official record about the wounds. Victor Bazanelle, in an interview, talks emotionally about Cedilena's pregnancy and the bayonet wounds. I ask myself if the bayonet wounds were the cause of her and the baby's death, or was her body mutilated after she died?[32]

Physicians who arrived on the site under flags of truce were driven back by bullets. The militia officers refused to allow doctors or Red Cross nurses to minister to the wounded. Dave Stuart, a young boy, spent Monday and that evening in a cellar. When he went to the depot to go to Trinidad, he and other boys, ten to twelve years old, were lined up against a wall and taunted by members of the militia. Railroad workers and passengers appealed to state officials to do something for the men, women, and children who were lying along the railroad tracks dead and wounded. Among those was Louis Tikas, whose battered body had been dumped along the railroad tracks. For two days, his body and that of James Fyler lay exposed. The fact that none of the bodies reported by railroad men could be found two days later was explained by the testimony of Mrs. Pearl Jolly.

Pearl Jolly, along with other women and children, had escaped to a farmhouse late the previous afternoon. She said that the next day, when the gunmen were looting the ruins of the tent colony, she also saw men gathering bodies and placing them in a huge pile. Then she watched them pour oil on the pile and burn the bodies. According to all accounts, there were more than fifty women and children missing, and it was believed that all traces of their murder were obliterated by the militia's burning of the funeral pyre.[33]

The front-page headline of the April 21, 1914, edition of *The Rocky Mountain News* read, "Thirteen Killed In Battle At Ludlow; Strikers' Tent Colony Burned." The newspaper covered the story for days and was the first to dub the tragedy the "Ludlow Massacre." That first article painted a horrific picture:

> Thirteen dead, scores injured, the Ludlow strikers' tent colony burned and hundreds of women and children homeless was the result up to midnight of one of the bloodiest battles in labor warfare in the West. Four hundred striking miners were entrenched in the hills back of Ludlow this morning awaiting daylight to wipe out 177 members of the state national guard, with whom they fought for fourteen hours yesterday.

John R. Lawson, a leader of the mine workers, went to Ludlow Monday and Tuesday to save the women and children, but the militia riddled his flag of truce and drove him back. William Snyder was coming from the tent colony Tuesday morning with his family, the body of his dead son cradled in one arm and his baby daughter in the other, when he was discovered by members of the militia. He, too, was taunted by the gunmen.

Another group of telephone repairmen arrived from Trinidad to repair the telephone lines. While walking along a dirt road toward Ludlow, they happened upon a little girl lying at the side of the roadway. Her head and upper torso had been badly burned. In one hand she held a doll. The other hand shielded the bright sunlight from her eyes. Just as one of the men was about to pick up the child, a militiaman approached the lineman and told him to leave the little girl where she was.[34] It is not known what became of the child, although it is commonly thought that she was burned to death in the pile of bodies set on fire by the militiamen.

Thirty women and children who escaped to the Powell Ranch were held as prisoners there until Tuesday night. They had nothing to eat or drink. Finally, Acting Governor Fitzgarrald (Governor Ammons being conveniently absent) ordered the release of the women and children. However, as the relief wagons made their way to the ranch house, Pearl Jolly, wearing a Red Cross insignia on her arm, ran out to meet it.

She was shot in the arm made prominent by the Red Cross band. Nevertheless, the women were finally rescued after the forty-eight-hour siege.[35]

On the evening of Tuesday, April 21, coffins carrying the bodies of the men killed by gunfire at Ludlow began arriving by wagon in Trinidad. The following day, Wednesday, April 22, a group of citizens carrying a Red Cross flag, including the Colorado labor commissioner, UMWA leader John McLennan, Ludlow survivor Pearl Jolly, local churchmen, nurses, railroad workers, miners' wives, reporters, and Trinidad photographer Lewis R. Dold, went to the tent colony site to inspect the ruins and retrieve bodies. Pearl Jolly thought she could assist in locating the place where it was presumed thirteen missing women and children lay. As members of the National Guard looked on and documented the scene with photographs, the group was led to where the telephone lineman had discovered the death pit cellar. In eerie silence, the group began carrying the dead out of the ground and onto wagons.

In subsequent days, funerals swamped Trinidad as mourners passed through the streets. On April 22, 1,500 people attended a service for the victims of the fire that included wagons carrying flower-laden caskets from the church to the cemetery. A week after the tragedy, a horse-drawn hearse transported the body of Louis Tikas to the graveyard, accompanied by 2,500 miners and their families.

A man stands aghast in the ruins of the Ludlow Colony. PHOTOGRAPH COURTESY OF THE NATIONAL ARCHIVES.

Women search the Ludlow camp for valuables to return to the families. PHOTOGRAPH BY THE BAIN NEWS SERVICE, COURTESY OF THE LIBRARY OF CONGRESS, LC-DIG-GGBAIN-15859.

Realizing that they had been betrayed by the state of Colorado and that they could hope to secure no protection from its militia, union men sent out an official call to arms, asking workers of the state and country to arm themselves and be ready to march at any minute. The fight would go on for another ten long days.

As the fighting continued in the coalfields of southern Colorado, 1,000 women in Denver marched to the state capitol on April 25 to protest conditions in the strike area and to demand that the governor request federal troops immediately. The *Denver Times* judged the action as "one of the most remarkable demonstrations by women which ever took place in this country." The women forced Governor Ammons to send a request directly to the president, to prevent the further murder of women and babies.

During those ten days of fighting, miners retaliated for the murders of their family members in a campaign that brought additional deaths and damage to mine facilities throughout Colorado's southern coalfields. But eventually federal troops restored order, and the strike ended in failure in December 1914.

The conflict at Ludlow on Monday, April 20, 1914, left twenty-one known dead and the tent colony a smoking ruin, rendering surviving colonists homeless and without possessions. Organizer Louis Tikas and two other union leaders, one member of the National Guard, one miner's eleven-year-old son, two strikers, and one young man merely passing through the area died as a result of gunfire. The deaths that shocked the national conscience, however, were those of the two women and eleven children who were asphyxiated and burned during the fire while seeking shelter in a tent cellar.

Several women who survived the Ludlow Massacre went on a speaking tour, garnering nationwide support for labor law reform. From left are Henrietta and Ben Lindsey, Pearl Jolly, Mary Petrucci, and Mary Thomas. (Judge Ben Lindsey was an outspoken advocate for the rights of children, women, and workers.) PHOTOGRAPH BY HARRIS & EWING, COURTESY OF THE LIBRARY OF CONGRESS, LC-DIG-HEC-04217.

The United Mine Workers eventually acquired the land encompassing the original tent colony and ceremonially dedicated the site. In 1918, the miner's union erected a monument to those who died at Ludlow. Labor union members consider the site, which drew national attention as a result of the tragedy, to be sacred ground. Molly Brown held several fundraisers in Denver and sent money, supplies, clothing, and even nurses to Ludlow.

The images and stories of the women and children who were killed or endured the attack are a testament to their courage and stamina in a time of complete horror. For example, Mary Thomas helped load rifles for the miners on that bloody day, while Pearl Jolly assisted Louis Tikas and tended to the injured. United by a common purpose and facing the same challenges, the inhabitants of the colony demonstrated surprising resilience and became what has been described as "a close-knit multinational community." Mary Thomas, looking back at the months she spent at Ludlow, had a profound sense of the time during the strike, writing, "The mine guards had lumped us together as being 'damn foreigners.' But we 'damn foreigners' became as one nationality. No one thought of anybody being different in color or national origin. We had become a family of world citizens."[36]

State Senator Helen Ring Robinson, who visited the colony during the strike, noticed the sense of cooperation and camaraderie among the tent inhabitants. Robinson observed, "Among the women, particularly, and many of the children, that this long winter had brought the nationalities together in a rather remarkable way. I saw the true melting pot at Ludlow."[37]

The tragedy of the Ludlow Massacre was not in vain. A clever media campaign led by *The Rocky Mountain News,* rather than the miners, included a nationwide speaking tour by women who survived the ordeal. Leading the women were Pearl Jolly and Mary Thomas. These courageous women, many of whom could barely speak English, managed to garner sympathy for their cause. As a result, labor laws changed not only in Colorado but across the nation. Years later, Mary Thomas looked back on that time in her life:

> Looking back now on those bitter days, I can see a wonderful thing in them despite the terror, the disappointments, the deprivations. Our suffering with the extreme cold and hunger had brought us all together. We had become a "family" of world citizens, petitioning for the right to make an honest living as free human beings.[38]

Mary Petrucci echoed those sentiments. She was in New York in 1915 for yet another investigation of the Ludlow Massacre when she was interviewed by the *New York Tribune:*

> Perhaps it seems strange to you that I want to go home, but I do. My man is there and my children are buried there. I have been so happy there. I used to sing around my work and playing with my babies. I'm 24 years old and I suppose I'll live a long time, but I don't see how I can ever be happy again. But you're not to think we could do it any differently another time. We are working people—my husband and I—and we're stronger than before the strike. I can't have my babies back. But perhaps when everybody knows about them, something will be done to make the world a better place for all babies.

Mary Harris "Mother" Jones

Mary Harris, better known as "Mother" Jones, the legendary labor activist and agitator, spent a good deal of time among the labor strikes throughout Colorado's mining towns.

Born Mary Harris in Cork County, Ireland, the date of her birth is uncertain, with various sources ranging from 1830 to 1837. Richard Harris, Mary's father, immigrated to America in 1835. Upon receiving his citizenship, he sent for his family in Ireland to join him. Harris found work with a railroad crew in Toronto, Canada, where Mary spent her formative years.

After receiving her teaching certificate at the age of twenty, Mary acquired her first teaching position at a convent in Monroe, Michigan. Now an adult alone in a new country, Mary quickly learned to be self-sufficient. After only eight months on the job, Mary quit and left Michigan for Chicago, Illinois, where she took up professional dressmaking. She later revealed that "I found I enjoyed making dresses better then bossing little children."[39]

Mary later moved to Memphis, Tennessee, where she met and married George Jones, an iron worker and staunch member of the local labor union. It was due to her husband's affiliations that Mary learned about the plight of laborers and the need for union representation. She also became keenly aware of the role of the wife in these situations and in life in general. She once said, "The wife must care for what the husband cares for, if he is to stay resolute."

The couple had four children before tragedy struck. During an epidemic of yellow fever, Mary's four children and her husband all succumbed to the deadly disease.

Now a widow, Mary Harris dressed in the traditional Victorian black dress of mourning. It was a look the five-foot-tall woman would embrace for the rest of her life. Mary returned to Chicago and resumed her dressmaking services. There she worked for some of the wealthiest families in Chicago. Predisposed to the plight of labor workers from her husband's unionist leanings, Mary became keenly aware of the labor struggles in Chicago. She later wrote, "I became wholly engrossed in the labor movement and in all the great industrial centers of the working men."

During the "Great Chicago Fire" of 1877, Mary lost her dress shop and her home. During her financial struggle to rebuild, Mary joined the Knights of Labor movement. It was during this time that Mary began supporting unemployed laborers, demanding jobs and leading marches from Washington, D.C., to Birmingham, Alabama.

Over time Mary became known for organizing the wives and children of the striking men. During a silk textile strike in Philadelphia, nearly 100,000 laborers, including some 16,000 children, left their jobs to strike, demanding the workweek be cut from sixty to fifty-five hours.

In June 1897, Mary gave a riveting speech and battle cry at a railway union convention in Pittsburgh. Admirers began to refer to her as "Mother" and the name stuck. From then on, Mary became Mother Jones to thousands of working men and women across the country.

In 1901, Mary was back in Pennsylvania where she organized the wives of the strikers. So effective was Mary that the district attorney in West Virginia named her "the most dangerous woman in America." In 1903, Mother Jones led a children's march with over 100 children from the textile mills of Philadelphia to New York City, leading the children all the way to President Theodore Roosevelt's home on Long Island. Just a few years later in 1905, she was one of the founding members of the Industrial Workers of the World.

Mother Jones was in West Virginia in 1912, where she was involved in what was known as the Paint Creek-Cabin coal miner's strike. Violence broke out between United Mine Workers and the mine owner's private security guards. Martial law was declared and Mother Jones was eventually arrested. She was accused by a military court of conspiracy to commit murder and was sentenced to twenty years in the state penitentiary. However, the incident caught the interest of the U.S. Congress, which began investigations into the conditions of the West Virginia coal mines. The findings were detrimental to many of the mine owners, and soon Mother Jones was released from her incarceration, pardoned by Governor Henry D. Hatfield.

Several mine owners were outraged and called on their state representatives to do something. On May 13, 1913, West Virginia Senator Nathan Goff Jr. took to the floor of the Senate and said:

> The name of "Mother Jones" has been brought into the controversy. Well, I have no fight with "Mother Jones." I am sorry that she feels aggrieved. If half the stories they tell about her in West Virginia in reference to this and other strikes there are true, she has certainly been—whatever else she may be; grand and good and a friend of the miners she may be—but she has certainly been inciting riot and urging insurrection. She does not deny it. She is the grandmother of them all; she takes pride in it; she is an expert; she is a good talker; she is effective in speaking to great audiences, naturally, she has influence with them.[40]

She was banished from more towns, arrested in many others. When Mother Jones heard of the atrocities committed during the miners strike at Ludlow, Colorado, she immediately left West Virginia and traveled to southern Colorado.

September 23, 1913, marked the beginning of one of the largest coal strikes in Colorado. The coal mines in southern Colorado were all owned by John D. Rockefeller Jr.'s Colorado Fuel & Iron Company. Miners were demanding an eight-hour workday, improved wages, and union recognition. Rockefeller refused to give in to their demands and hired the Baldwin-Felts Detective Agency; its members were actually hired guns expected to intimidate the miners and shut down the strike.

Mother Jones arrived in Trinidad and made it her base of operations. After making contacts and learning the particulars of the situation, she set off for the coal mining tent camp of Ludlow. There she organized the women not only to protest, but to aid their husbands during the strike. In doing so Mother Jones became a strong role model for the mining camp women.

In early January 1914, Mother Jones was arrested in Trinidad for inciting a riot on the steps of the post office. She had been rallying supporters of the strike

In 1914, Mother Jones' image was carried by newspapers across the country. PHOTOGRAPH BY THE BAIN NEWS SERVICE, COURTESY OF THE LIBRARY OF CONGRESS, LC-DIG-GGBAIN-1597.

and gave a fiery speech that included strong statements such as, "If they want to hang me, let them hang me. But when I am on the scaffold, I'll cry, 'Freedom for the working class!'"[41]

General John Chase of the Colorado State Militia allowed Mother Jones no visitors and no books or newspapers in her cell, and she remained under heavy guard. She later highlighted the incongruity of her imprisonment, saying, "Five big burly uniformed murderers with their guns on their shoulders and a belt of bullets around their stomachs and a saber hanging to their sides came up every night at six o'clock to put in twenty-four hours watching an old woman 84 years of age."[42]

Eventually the very women Mother Jones came to help during the strike rallied to help her. On January 21, 1914, nearly 1,000 women, many with their children in tow, marched in protest on the streets of Trinidad. At the same time, Colorado University professor James Brewster exclaimed, "The arrest of Mother Jones without a warrant, without any suspicion of crime, was one of the greatest outrages upon civilized American jurisprudence. Has it come to this that men so fear the truth that they must unlawfully imprison and silence this woman?"[43]

In Trinidad, women marched to protest Mother Jones' arrest and imprisonment. One carries a sign reading, "God Bless Mother Jones." PHOTOGRAPH COURTESY OF DENVER PUBLIC LIBRARY, SPECIAL COLLECTIONS.

When the protesters ignored an order to disperse, a militia officer ordered the soldiers to charge. The resulting skirmish infuriated the public, and the outcry forced officials to release Mother Jones from jail. General Chase warned her to never show up in Trinidad again.

Mother Jones defied Chase time and time again. On one occasion in front of hundreds of protesters, she demanded that John D. Rockefeller Jr. leave the comfort of his New York office and come west so that he might see for himself the deplorable conditions in the Colorado coal mines.

As for the miners, Mother Jones assured them that their wives were very much a part of their struggle. At Ludlow, she worked directly with the women and children. If she ever truly earned her nickname it was at Ludlow. She cared for the sick, nursed the invalid, washed clothes, cooked meals, and read to the children. Mother Jones rallied the women and urged them to fight alongside their husbands with speeches such as this:

> It is not the demonstration or violence or the speeches that will win this strike, if it is won, but the simple continuity of feeding and washing and cleaning that goes on between those canvas walls, those trips along the muddy paths between the wash lines and the coal piles and the store. And if the women give up one day on the scrimping and hoarding and patching and say they've had enough, then the strike is lost.[44]

Then, in early April, Mother Jones was called to Washington, D.C., to testify before Congress on the conditions of the coal miners and the brutality of the mine owners in particular. In her usual fiery style, Mother Jones declared, "Tis an outrage indeed that Rockefeller should own the coal that God put in the earth for all the people."[45]

Meanwhile, back in Colorado, tension between the militia and the striking miners was reaching its peak. Then, on the morning of April 20, 1914, all hell broke loose, sparking the Ludlow Massacre. Still smoldering at sunrise the following morning, the horrible carnage lay before all to see. Twenty people were dead, mostly women and children. All the miners of southern Colorado were outraged and even more determined to fight together against the militia. So began a ten-day war. Mother Jones hurried back to Colorado to help her beloved miners, arriving in time to attend nearly all of the funerals and mourning alongside the grief-stricken women.

In the end, the Colorado coal strike was for naught and was a huge defeat for the labor union. But Mother Jones continued her crusade for the common working man and woman.

Friends and supporters celebrated Mother Jones' 100th birthday in 1930. PHOTOGRAPH COURTESY OF THE LIBRARY OF CONGRESS, LC-USZ62-50378.

In 1924, she wrote her autobiography detailing her many attempts as righting the wrongs perpetrated on the working class as she saw it. She lived long enough to see Congress enact child labor laws, and that at least was some progress.

Toward the end of her life, Mother Jones lived on the Maryland farm of friends Water and Lillie May Burgess. There, on May 1, 1930, she enjoyed a huge party thrown for her alleged 100th birthday. Throughout her life, Mother Jones often fibbed about her age. When she was younger, she said she was older, and when she was older, she claimed she was younger. And when she was even older, she said she was much older. In any case, her birthday celebration was covered in all the major newspapers and cards and letters poured in.

Even her one-time nemesis, John D. Rockefeller Jr., sent a telegram, which read, "Please accept my heartiest congratulations on your 100th birthday. Your loyalty to your ideals, your fearless adherence to your duty as you have seen it, is an inspiration to all who have known you."[46]

To which the fiery crusader retorted, "Well, he's a damn good sport, anyway. We surely had some bitter battles. But it was kind of him to remember me, but hell, I can't do him or anyone any harm for I'm out of the running now."[47]

Mary Harris "Mother" Jones, with her work done, died peacefully in her sleep on November 30, 1930. ✦

Notes

1. Clyne, Rick J. *Coal People: Life in Southern Colorado's Company Towns, 1890–1930.* Colorado Historical Society, 2000. p. 83.
2. "Testimonies and Memories: Voices From the Ludlow Massacre Survive." Historical marker erected by United Mine Workers of America in Ludlow, junction of County Highways 44 and 61.5. Transcript at Denver University Library Archives.
3. ibid. p. 89.
4. ibid. p. 90.
5. "Ludlow Tent Colony Site," p. 59. National Register of Historic Places Registration.
6. Thomas, Mary. *Those Damn Foreigners.* Minerva Books, 1971.
7. "Ludlow Tent Colony Site." National Register of Historic Places Registration.
8. ibid.
9. ibid.
10. McGovern, George S. and Leonard F. Guttridge. *The Great Coalfield War.* University Press of Colorado, 1996. p. 105.
11. Thomas. *Those Damn Foreigners,* p. 106.
12. "Testimonies and Memories: Voices From the Ludlow Massacre Survive." UMWA historical marker, Denver University Library Archives.
13. Clyne, *Coal People,* p. 42.
14. ibid.
15. Clyne, *Coal People,* p. 87.
16. Papanikolas, Zeese. *Buried Unsung: Louis Tikas and the Ludlow Massacre.* University of Nebraska Press, 1991. p. 163.
17. Jolly, Pearl. "Under Fire in the Ludlow Tent Colony, 1914." In *Violence in the West: The Johnson County War and the Ludlow Massacre, A Brief History with Documents.* Marilynn S. Johnson. Waveland Press, 2014. p. 131.
18. Thomas. *Those Damn Foreigners,* p. 114.
19. Moore, Marat. *Women in the Mines: Stories of Life and Work.* Twayne Publishing, 1996.
20. McGovern and Guttridge, *The Great Coalfield War,* p. 216.
21. "Ludlow Tent Colony Site," National Register of Historic Places Registration.
22. "Testimonies and Memories: Voices From the Ludlow Massacre Survive." Denver University Library Archives.

23. *The Colorado Coal Miner's Strike: Industrial Relations: Final Report and Testimony Submitted to Congress.* Washington, D.C., U.S. Government Printing Office, 1916.
24. McGovern and Guttridge, *The Great Coalfield War,* p. 115.
25. Register of Historic Places Registration Form.
26. ibid.
27. This was tent #58, which became an incinerator as the fire raged.
28. The Military Investigations Committee did not deny that the battle was premeditated and planned. It also found that the militia set fire to the tents with gasoline and matches. Although accounts of the events of the massacre differ, some aspects are corroborated in various written versions.
29. "Testimonies and Memories: Voices From the Ludlow Massacre Survive." Denver University Library Archives.
30. "Ludlow Tent Colony Site," p. 45. National Register of Historic Places Registration.
31. *Denver Express,* April 21, 1914.
32. Montoya, Fawn-Amber and Karin Larkin. *Communities of Ludlow: Collaborative Stewardship and the Ludlow Centennial Commemoration Commission.* University Press of Colorado, 2022. pp. xxxiv–xxxv.
33. *The Colorado Coal Miner's Strike: Industrial Relations: Final Report and Testimony Submitted to Congress.* Washington, D.C., U.S. Government Printing Office, 1916.
34. ibid.
35. Jolly. "Under Fire in the Ludlow Tent Colony, 1914." p. 146.
36. Thomas. *Those Damn Foreigners,* p. 148.
37. "Ludlow Tent Colony Site," p. 88. National Register of Historic Places Registration.
38. Thomas. *Those Damn Foreigners.*
39. Jones, Mary Harris. *The Autobiography of Mother Jones.* Dover Publications, 2012.
40. Report of the West Virginia Mining Investigation Commission, August 28, 1913.
41. Atkinson, Linda. *Mother Jones, the Most Dangerous Woman in America.* Crown Publishing, 1978. p. 7.
42. Steel, Edward M., ed. *The Correspondence of Mother Jones.* University of Pittsburgh Press, 1985. p. 89.
43. ibid.
44. Papanikolas, *Buried Unsung: Louis Tikas and the Ludlow Massacre,* p. 163.
45. Jones. *Autobiography of Mother Jones,* p. 115.
46. Ruby, Lois. *Strike! Mother Jones and the Colorado Coal Field War.* Filter Press, 2012. p. 164.
47. ibid.

5

THE SILVERY SAN JUANS

HIGH IN THE CREVICES OF THIS MOUNTAIN RANGE, the San Juan River is born. It is from its flowing waters that gold was discovered. Mining riches provided economic stability to the region, and railroads brought much-needed relief from the isolation of such a mountain wonderland.

But it is silver in particular that the San Juan region is known for. So much so that a town was named for the mighty ore: Silverton.

Some of the richest mines were located high above the towns of Telluride, Ouray, Creede, and Lake City. Mines such as the Tomboy, the Smuggler, and Camp Bird became legends. Books and songs were written about them. Legends, lore, and ore are what the San Juan Mountains are known for.

Perched high above timberline on sheer rugged cliffs almost touching the sky are the ghost towns of the mines and cabins where miners worked and lived. They remain a testament to the hard mountain life. In winter, snow depths often exceed twenty feet, with snowslides and avalanches a common occurrence. But Harriet Backus endured and came to cherish her time high above Telluride at the Tomboy Mine.

Nearby, the town of Silverton had a large population of miners and their families. Mine owners, too, lived here. Nearly everyone owned a claim or two, and the lucky ones got rich.

Along the Uncompahgre River, prospectors found ore with good color. Following the river upriver, they discovered rich silver veins near the mouth of Canyon Creek. This would later become the townsite of Ouray. No mine was more famous than the Camp Bird Mine perched high above Ouray. It made Thomas Walsh the district's first millionaire and produced roughly $27 million in gold. It would also provide a luxurious lifestyle for Walsh's daughter, Evalyn.

Otto Mears turned his mountain toll roads into railbeds and brought the railroad to the mines. His daughter Cora would become president of his railroad empire, one of the first female railroad presidents in the country.

OURAY

Evalyn Walsh McLean: Daddy's Little Rich Girl

A young Evalyn poses for a portrait with her father, Thomas Walsh.
PHOTOGRAPH COURTESY OF THE LIBRARY OF CONGRESS, LC-USZ62-119018.

She had it all: wealth, power, prestige, glitz, and glamour. She risked it all to own the world's largest blue diamond—the Hope Diamond—and some would say the curse that came with it. Many people believed in the supposed curse and blamed the diamond for the tragedies in Evalyn's life.

Evalyn Walsh enjoyed the finer things that accrued from being the daughter of a wealthy mining tycoon. PHOTOGRAPH COURTESY OF THE LIBRARY OF CONGRESS, LC-USZ62-123723.

But not Evalyn Walsh McLean. In her autobiography, aptly titled *Father Struck It Rich,* Evalyn blamed her misfortunes on wealth in general, not one particular gemstone.

Evalyn Lucille Walsh was born on August 1, 1886. She was the first child of Thomas and Carrie Walsh. Thomas was an Irish immigrant who arrived in America through New York City in 1869. He was a carpenter by trade and had been an apprentice in Lisronagh, Tipperary, Ireland since the age of twelve.

In America, Thomas Walsh ventured west in 1870 where his carpentry skills were in great need. He soon caught "gold fever" and followed the horde of hopeful prospectors to the Black Hills of South Dakota. Returning to Colorado with a $75,000 purse, Walsh settled in Leadville where he met and married Carrie Bell Reed on July 11, 1879. The couple operated the Grand Central Hotel in Leadville, but the gold fever never left Walsh. At night he studied mining technology and quickly became an expert in the field.

Thomas Walsh took a methodical approach to mining and investing. He invested in several mines in the Leadville area and reinvested his earnings in other promising properties. One of those investments led to development of the Camp

Thomas Walsh's Camp Bird Mine produced vast amounts of gold ore. PHOTOGRAPH BY RUSSELL LEE, COURTESY OF THE LIBRARY OF CONGRESS, LC-DIG-FSAC-1A34180.

Bird Mine high above Ouray in the San Juans where he discovered an enormous gold vein in 1896. According to Evalyn, her mother was away visiting family at the time. Her father was so excited about the discovery that he burst into Evalyn's room and exclaimed, "Daughter, I've struck it rich!"[1]

Suddenly Evalyn's world changed. Her parents whisked her off to a world of wealth, travel, and glamour. She had new store-bought dresses, shoes, coats, and hats. Money was no object. Evalyn was afforded a lavish lifestyle and she wasted no time taking advantage.

Meanwhile, the Camp Bird Mine was producing an average of $5,000 a day in ore, bankrolling the Walshes' lifestyle. Evalyn attended private schools in America and Europe. She was a distinguished guest in France and was greeted by royalty from Austria to England, all while still a child.

Back in America, Evalyn eagerly awaited the completion of her father's million-dollar mansion she dubbed the "2020." It was being built in the finest neighborhood in Washington, D.C., at 2020 Massachusetts Avenue. When it was finished, Evalyn marveled at its splendor: "A canopy of blue satin over my bed filled me each time I awakened with the realization that life had changed for Evalyn Walsh.

Evalyn relished the magnificence of the family's mansion at 2020 Massachusetts Avenue in Washington, D.C.
PHOTOGRAPH BY JACK BOUCHER, COURTESY OF THE LIBRARY OF CONGRESS, HABS DC,WASH,209—1.

The figured blue satin that covered the walls did not lull me; it was as a signal for me to get up quickly, to put on one of my new frocks, to live." Evalyn later recalled the first dinner party her parents gave shortly after moving to America's political capital. Her mother was very self-conscious in her first evening gown. Her father, on the other hand, was completely comfortable among his new and powerful friends.

At one such party, the guests included a prominent publisher, John R. McLean, his wife, Emily, and their ne'er-do-well son, Edward. (Years later, writer Lucius Beebe would describe young Edward as "spoiled as a mackerel three hours in the sun."[2]) Evalyn recalled first meeting Edward:

> Mrs. McLean introduced me to some and then she brought her son to me. She called him "Neddie." We were both eleven, but he was a gawky creature so extraordinarily tall he seemed more like fourteen. His mother enjoined him to take me to dinner, and to my surprise he obeyed her. I really was in terror, because I had been cautioned against a myriad of blunders I might make. There was a confusing array of silver on each side of my plate. Somebody spoke to me in raillery [teasing] and I burst into tears.

To repair her embarrassment and bruised ego, Evalyn resorted to asking daddy for whimsical things she felt she just had to have. And she was getting pretty good at it. Evalyn later wrote:

> I had become aware that if Mother so much as breathed a wish for anything—even a set of $1,800 furs from Gunther's—she got it, overnight at the latest. Probably that is how I got my idea that walking to school was a little trying for my dignity. At any rate, I went to Father's room and found him standing before a small round mirror, his face covered with lather. I was forbidden to touch the razor or to talk with him when it was actually touching his face. So it was while he turned with the utmost care and concentration to slide it back and forth over the glossy surface of his strop that I put him to a test like the one to which Aladdin subjected the slave of his lamp. "Papa. do you think you could afford to hire a horse and carriage for me to ride to school sometimes?" I saw creases forming in the mask of white soap under his nose and around his mouth, and he began to laugh heartily. He laughed so much I was chagrined; then he sobered and began stropping his razor once more. "Darling, I guess I can manage to rent you a horse and carriage."

Tom Walsh's star was rising among the social and political elite in the nation's capital. He joined the exclusive Metropolitan Club of Washington, his sponsor being Secretary of State John Hay. Hay's wife, Clara, recommended Evalyn to the elite Dobbs Ferry Girls School. "An agreement was reached whereby I would attend the school and study—music, French and other parlor tricks of ladies. By some school magic, I was to become a lady!"

High society does have its privileges. Earlier in 1902, Thomas Walsh donated gold from his Camp Bird Mine for the badges at the launching of the U.S. Navy's newest vessel, the USS *Denver*. In return, later the same year, Walsh's good friend Senator Henry Teller selected Evalyn Walsh to christen the new battleship, the USS *Colorado*. The choice was criticized in the editorial pages of the *Denver Post*. Many thought the governor's daughter, Cora Peabody, deserved the honor. But Senator Teller was adamant. Nevertheless, Walsh "cheerfully, willingly, and of my own volition" withdrew Evalyn's name from consideration.

Evalyn's mother thought her fourteen-year-old daughter was old enough to wear her hair in a more mature style. As with many mother-daughter relationships, Evalyn was dead-set against her mother's wishes. It took her father—and a bit of coaxing—to get Evalyn to behave. She told the story this way:

> At last my father spoke to me. "Listen, the thing you want more than all else in the world, I think, is a diamond ring. I'm right?" "You surely are, my daddy!" I replied. I was flip when I was going on fifteen. "Well then, if you will wear your hair back off your ears as other nice girls do, I will give you such a diamond ring as will make you quite the envy of all your friends."
>
> I thought he had the ring in his pocket then, but he shook his head and said, "First fix your hair." It was an awful pull for me to give up what I truly thought was my personality, but I did it and that was how I got the first of all my jewels.

Evalyn never seemed to shy away from her girlish antics, even at the age of sixteen when she managed to snag a proposal from Ned McLean. Evalyn wrote:

> My first proposal came soon after that—brought on, I now suspect, because I kept the ring in sight and quite a mystery. My papa's gift? How quite absurd I made those dancing school companions seem who suggested such a thing. I sneaked out of the class to ride with gawky Ned McLean in his back-firing motor-car. Not many boys had automobiles then, nor old folks either, but his parents gave him anything he wanted. We rolled along and crossed a bridge.
>
> I saw Ned watching me and I observed the black down on his upper lip that could soon become a moustache. Just then he blurted out, "I think you ought to marry me."
>
> Well, I didn't know what to say. I felt a swelling in my mind that was a sense of triumph. After this, I knew, I could not fail; without half-trying I had caught a man. So naturally I did not say no to him, but neither did I say yes.

While on a family trip to Ireland, a strange thing happened. Or was it an omen of things to come for Evalyn? She later recalled the incident:

> We were on our way to Queenstown when what I speak of happened. In the twilight of our train compartment I became aware that this lovely woman on board was drunk. There was something else wrong, but I did not know quite

how to define the trouble. Father, I could see plainly, was provoked. Then we reached our station. Just then I whirled around. Father, swearing, was bending over. The woman had fallen flat. A misty or foggy night will evoke that scene in my mind as long as I live. They got some black coffee for her and she began talking. Father had made wrathful by a rebuke, and by this time she was not in the least beautiful; disordered hair made her hag like.

"Tom Walsh!" She spoke his name with sober fury.

"I want to tell you something." Her eyes roved from one face to another until she fixed her gaze on me.

"Tom Walsh I curse Evalyn. I want you before you're dead to see her in the gutter."

It was all said quietly, and no other person spoke.

Evalyn was close with her brother, Vinson, looking dapper here circa 1900. PHOTOGRAPH COURTESY OF THE LIBRARY OF CONGRESS, LC-USZ62-119013.

August 19, 1905, was a terrible day for Evalyn and one she would never get over. She had let her brother, Vinson, drive her beloved red Mercedes sports car, a gift from her father. Evalyn was in the passenger seat when suddenly the car jolted and, according to Evalyn, began to "swerve, sway and pitch." A rear tire had blown and the car swerved into the post of a bridge. Evalyn recalled:

> I kept conscious until I saw my mother. I tried to tell her Vinson was in better condition than I was but had been taken to the hospital. I did not know it then, of course, but he died about the time I was placed in the ambulance. The fact of his death was kept from me.

> I finally learned that Vin was dead. They gave me morphine whenever I had need of it. And I needed it for pain of all kinds.

Help came from an unexpected source—Evalyn's on-again, off-again boyfriend, Ned McLean. Ned appealed to his father, John McLean, the owner and publisher of the very influential *Washington Post*. Through his many connections, the elder McLean was able to obtain the services of a highly rated doctor at Johns Hopkins, Dr. John Miller Finny. The doctor operated on Evalyn's leg. When it was over, the good news was that she would walk again. The bad news was she was becoming addicted to morphine. Finally, after seeing her father in tears, Evalyn sought help for her addiction.

Evalyn seemed to harbor some sort of disdain for her incorrigible boyfriend. Here is her version of the relationship:

> I was the only living human who ever exercised control over Ned McLean. Certainly he never ruled himself. His father was limp and spineless where his only son was concerned. His mother, Emily Beale McLean, was the leader of Washington society, but she never was able to give her son any of that courage with which the Beales were so richly endowed; all Ned received from that part of his heritage was recklessness in dissipation.
>
> In a measure, I seemed able to strengthen Ned.

The couple were married in Denver on July 22, 1908. Evalyn wrote a rather humorous account of her wedding:

> One afternoon in late July—it was the twenty-second—while we were driving miles from Denver in my car, attended by a chauffeur and Maggie Buggy, Ned said a reckless thing—"Let's get married." Precisely because it was a daring thought, I liked it. I agreed. Ned went into some store that had a telephone, to call up Crawford Hill. After just a little coaxing Crawford said he would fix everything and meet us, with a ring and a license, with Louise, his wife, and with Colonel Billy Stapleton, at St. Mark's Episcopal Church. That day I was wearing a dress of white broadcloth and a high straw hat thickly feathered with snowy ostrich plumes. Ned was wearing a light grey serge suit and a cloth cap.
>
> The next thing was our return to Wolhurst; as our car turned into the tree-bordered, gravel driveway I was aware of being grateful that father was away. Mother was not pleased but was pleasant.

The honeymoon began at the Antlers Hotel in Colorado Springs followed by a trip abroad, capped by the first time Evalyn laid eyes on the infamous Hope Diamond. Evalyn wrote, "Ned and I decided that we would not have a honeymoon unless we went roaming over Europe. Our fathers matched each other in extravagance and gave us each $100,000."

On a honeymoon shopping spree in Paris, the McLeans stopped by to see the famed jeweler, Pierre Cartier. Cartier showed the couple the spectacular blue Hope Diamond. Evalyn revealed the details of the event, writing, "'We have just the thing for you,' said one of the firm. Then he hypnotized me by showing me an ornament that made bright spots before my eyes. (Anyway, that's what I told my father later.)"

As if on cue, Cartier proceeded to tell Evalyn of the legendary curse the spectacular gem held. In 1668, a French gem merchant named Jean-Baptiste Tavernier smuggled a 112.1875-carat, rough, blue-colored diamond out of India and sold it to King Louis XIV, whose court jeweler cut it into a 67.125-carat finished gem. Legend has it that Tavernier was later torn apart by wild dogs (in reality, he died at age eighty-four of natural causes). The diamond's curse was also said to have led to the beheading of King Louis XVI and his queen, Marie Antoinette, during the French Revolution. (In fact, the diamond was no longer under French ownership by then, having traveled to England after the death of Louis XIV.) In 1830, a diamond dealer, Daniel Eliason, offered a large 67.125-carat, blue diamond for sale in London. Henry Philip Hope, a London banker, bought the diamond. Upon Henry's death, the diamond, now named the Hope, went to his nephew, Henry Thomas Hope, as part of his inheritance. Soon the Hope family allegedly suffered a series of tragic deaths and financial ruin; thus the myth of the curse continued.

In any case, the McLeans left the jewelry shop without the diamond. But Evalyn was smitten. Back in America, the McLeans settled into their new home in Bar Harbor, purchased for them by Tom Walsh. They were also given an allowance of $1,000 a month, but the money never lasted the thirty days.

In the summer of 1911, Cartier reset the diamond, thinking it would better appeal to Evalyn's taste. He set off for America to meet with the gold heiress and show her his new masterpiece. Once in America, he dashed off a note to the McLeans:

> Dear Sir,
>
> We have the pleasure to inform you that Mr. Pierre Cartier has arrived from Europe this morning on the *Lusitania*. He has brought with him the Hope diamond and the documents concerning the Hope diamond. He has a book

written by Tavernier himself, who, if you remember, sold the stone to King Louis XIV.

Mr. Pierre Cartier will be glad to be honoured with an appointment, so as to be able to give you all required details.

Awaiting your kind answer,
We beg to remain, dear sir,
Yours respectfully,
Cartier[3]

Cartier called on the McLeans at their new home and showed Evalyn the reset diamond. He then left it on her nightstand for the weekend. "Objects unlucky for others are lucky for me," Evalyn told a friend. When the weekend ended, a sales contract was drawn up for $180,000, payable in installments. The contract included the following clause: "Should any fatality occur to the family of Edward B. McLean within six months, the said Hope Diamond is agreed to be exchanged for jewelry of equal value."[4]

With money as no object, Evalyn splurged on jewelry, including strings of pearls and the Hope Diamond, shown here in 1914. PHOTOGRAPH COURTESY OF THE LIBRARY OF CONGRESS, LC-USZ62-71454.

Ned McLean's mother died six months later, and the McLeans, in turn, stopped payments to Cartier. After some months, Cartier brought suit against the McLeans for breach of contract, claiming the elder Mrs. McLean's death occurred outside the six-month time frame specified in the sales contract. The case dragged on for years, but in the end the McLeans lost. They were ordered to resume payments as well as pay an astounding $26,000 in interest.

After the death of her mother-in-law and the bad luck fallout from the lawsuit, Evalyn had the Hope Diamond blessed by Catholic Monsignor Russell. After the blessing, a tree in the church courtyard was struck by lightning and came crashing down. Regarding the cursed gem, Evalyn told a friend, "The luckiest thing about it is that if I ever had to, I could hock it."

And hock it she did. Over and over again. Evalyn had a habit of ordering things, from clothes to automobiles, catered parties to expensive jewelry. Yet she never seemed to have the money to pay the bills. So the bedazzling blue jewel would be hocked time and again.

When it wasn't hocked, Evalyn wore it nearly everywhere. For lavish parties she liked to pair it with her 94.8-carat Star of the East diamond or her 31.2-carat McLean diamond. Her friend Alice Roosevelt Longworth loved to describe Evalyn's glitz and glamour for the newspaper's society pages. It was all second nature to Evalyn, as she wrote:

> Because of our wealth, the rich scenes in which my husband and I moved were peopled with the great, and the powerful, of our generation. When any one of these might wish to meet his kind at play around Washington, a likely place to make the contact was our country estate—my home, which we call Friendship, and which has been a piece of the capital.

Tragedy struck the McLean household once again in the spring of 1919. Ned and Evalyn were in Louisville, Kentucky, attending the Kentucky Derby, when they received word that their oldest child, Vinson Walsh McLean, had died. The nine-year-old boy had darted out into the street and was struck by an automobile.

Evalyn was grief-stricken and for a time returned to her morphine habit. She and Ned began to fight. Constantly. Eventually, Evalyn managed to kick her habit, but Ned's drinking continued. He was caught entertaining President Warren Harding's cabinet members with prostitutes. In another incident, also involving prostitutes, Ned took a circus bear to a house of ill repute in Palm Beach, Florida.[5]

Evalyn and her husband Ned, shown here with their son Jock, hobnobbed with the political elite, including Florence and President Warren Harding. PHOTOGRAPH COURTESY OF THE LIBRARY OF CONGRESS, LC-DIG-PPM-SCA-10434.

Evalyn had had enough and filed for divorce. To cover up the embarrassment, the McLean family had Ned committed to a sanitarium in Baltimore, Maryland. The McLean family settled the divorce, paying Evalyn $7,500 a month for alimony and maintenance.

Meanwhile, Evalyn's daughter, Evalyn Washington McLean, had married fifty-seven-year-old Senator Robert Reynolds, a North Carolina Democrat who had once courted her mother.

During the Great Depression, financial strain overcame the McLean household. The trustees of the McLean holdings reduced Evalyn's alimony amount when the family newspapers, the *Cincinnati Enquirer* and the *Washington Post,* were losing subscribers. Finally, the newspaper entities were sold at auction. The *Washington Post* was bought by the Meyer family and would be run eventually by their daughter, Katherine Graham.

In the 1930s, a spate of kidnappings targeted children of the wealthy. Evalyn again hocked her Hope Diamond in 1932 when the infant son of her friends, Charles and Anne Morrow Lindbergh, was kidnapped. The sale raised $100,000, which

Evalyn gave to Gaston Means, a former FBI agent and convicted felon who claimed to know where the baby was. But Means wasn't involved in the kidnapping; he simply took advantage of the situation and scammed the Lindberghs and Evalyn. Means was prosecuted and sentenced to fifteen years in prison. Evalyn later wrote:

> Why should I have tried to get the Lindbergh baby back to its mother? Well, for one thing I had lived more than a score of years haunted daily by the fear of just what had happened to the Lindberghs. So many people were then wishing they might save the baby and revenge the crime that I wonder why so many persons now ask me what prompted me to involve myself in the hunt.

Evalyn had more tragedy to deal with. Edward "Ned" McLean died in a mental institution in July 1941. Then in September 1946, Evalyn's namesake daughter died of an overdose of sleeping pills. It seems Evalyn may have grown weary of all the tragedy.

In 1936, Evalyn Walsh McLean published her memoir, Father Struck It Rich. *PHOTOGRAPH COURTESY OF THE LIBRARY OF CONGRESS, LC-DIG-HEC-40377.*

Less than a year after her daughter's death, Evalyn contracted pneumonia and died in Washington, D.C., on April 26, 1947. Evalyn Lucille Walsh McLean was sixty years old.

Following her death, J. Edgar Hoover, director of the FBI, took charge of Evalyn's jewelry, including the Hope Diamond, locking the cache away in an FBI safe. Years later, Harry Winston, a New York City jeweler, bought several pieces, including the Hope Diamond. In 1958, Winston donated the diamond to the Smithsonian Institution where it remains today. The Hope Diamond is displayed in a shatterproof glass case, safe from harm, and if the curse is to be believed, where it can do no harm.

Evalyn once said, "The problem with wealth; it is unearthed in undisciplined hands."

Was that the root cause of Evalyn Walsh McLean's many tragedies? Or was it the curse of the Hope Diamond?

RIDGEWAY

Cora Mears Pitcher: The Pathfinder's Daughter

One of the first women to become president of a railroad company, Cora Mears Pitcher not only guided her father's railroad company to new heights—literally—in the rich San Juan Mining District, she also kept her father's legacy alive.

Cora Emma Mears was the third daughter born to Otto and Mary Kampfshulte Mears. Otto Mears was born in May 1840 in Kurland, Russia. He was orphaned at three years old when both of his parents died of disease. Eventually he was sent to America to live with relatives. At eleven years old, Otto was forced to work for his room and board and had never attended school. But at nineteen years old, Otto became a U.S. citizen. When the Civil War broke out, he enlisted with the California Volunteers and saw action under his commanding officer, Christopher "Kit" Carson. The two became close friends, and Otto enjoyed Carson's descriptions of Colorado.

Following the war, Otto left for Colorado, eventually settling in the relatively isolated San Luis Valley. He dabbled in farming for a time before turning to cattle to make a living. But he needed roads to get the cattle to other markets.

Mears set out to improve a path over Poncha Pass, turning it into a very profitable toll road by November 1870. This was the first good road connecting the San Luis and Arkansas Valleys. It was also the first of many successful roadways Mears would build. Next, Mears acquired an interest in the Saguache and San Juan Toll

Road Company and began building a route from Saguache over Cochetopa Pass. Thirty-year-old Mears was instrumental in establishing the town of Saguache and in November 1870 was married there to thirty-two-year old Mary Kampfshulte, an immigrant from Germany. The couple would have three daughters: Laura May, born in 1872; Eva, who died in infancy in 1876; and Cora Emma, born in 1879.

By 1873, when silver had been discovered in the San Juan Mountains, Mears was again building roads, this time to the rich silver mines in the Red Mountain Mining District. Mears' reputation for building roads where no one thought it was possible earned him the name, "Pathfinder of the San Juans." And so he was. Mears had an uncanny ability for finding passable routes, transforming the impossible to the possible.

Thanks to his work ethic and integrity, Otto Mears, seen here in 1880 with Ouray, chief of the Colorado Utes, served for a time as an interpreter and negotiator with the Ute tribe. PHOTOGRAPH COURTESY OF DENVER PUBLIC LIBRARY, SPECIAL COLLECTIONS.

Mears had been considering a toll road to the mines in the San Juans, but with quick and ever-changing mining developments and the very real promise of a railroad connection, Mears turned to railroad building. His narrow toll road from Ouray over Red Mountain Pass to Silverton became his first railbed. Begun in 1881, the road crept along beautiful creeks and through deep canyons. Because of the incredible scenery, it was soon known as the "Rainbow Route," so named by David Day, Ouray newspaper owner and Mears' best friend. By the summer of 1883,

Mears' narrow gauge railroad had reached Silverton. In his *Solid Muldoon* newspaper, David Day editorialized:

> Five weeks ago, where Red Mountain now stands was a woodland mesa covered with heavy spruce timber. Today, hotels, printing offices, groceries, meat markets, a telephone office, saloons and dance houses are up and booming; the blast is heard on every side and prospectors can be seen snowshoeing in every direction.

The narrow gauge Silverton Railroad was incorporated on July 5, 1887.[6] However, it was a different toll road turned railbed and auto highway, linking Silverton with Ouray, that endeared Otto Mears to nearly everyone in the San Juan Mountains for decades to come. Today it is known as the "Million Dollar Highway," and the reasons are legendary. Some say it was so named for the rich ore-laden gravel blasted to create the road. Others say it is named for the spectacular scenery, worth a million dollars, and still others say it was the cost to build the eighteen-mile road. All three have merit and are plausible. In any case, the route was an engineering marvel, complete with steep inclines and hairpin curves, and was unmatched by any other mountain railroad.

Mears followed with the Rio Grande Southern Railroad, which ran 162 miles from Ridgway to Durango, over Lizard Pass at over 10,000 feet above sea level, and the legendary Ophir Loop with a set of wooden trestles, some almost 100 feet high.[7] In partnership with Simon Guggenheim, the rails were laid along the Animas River. Mears told the railroad workers, "Put your line right down the wheel ruts. I built the road, I guess I can lay track on it if I want to."[8]

The *San Juan Democrat* editorialized on the coming of the railroad, writing, "The Pathfinder's Iron Horse will shortly invade the tranquil precincts of Howardsville and Mayor Appel is preparing a speech which he will unload on the suffering but patient public."

The January 1, 1892, *Rico Sun* newspaper noted, "[T]he Rio Grande Southern Railroad's new rotary snowplows passed Rico this morning on its way to the Arctic region near Telluride."

Mears' next project was extending the rail lines of the Silverton, Gladstone & Northern Railroad. Otto Mears' railroads allowed for the ease of ore transportation from the San Juan mines. Everybody got rich. That is until the silver crash of 1893, when the price of silver plummeted and silver mines all over Colorado ceased operations almost overnight. With the highest concentration of silver mines in the San Juans, this area was particularly hit hard and so was Otto Mears' railroad empire.

In 1892, Otto Mears gave his daughter Cora a gold-filagree lifetime railroad pass for his Rio Grande Southern and Silverton lines. PHOTOGRAPH COURTESY OF HISTORY COLORADO, 99.270.1240.379.

He was forced to liquidate much of his holdings. He held on to his railroads, which were now in receivership. Expansion was out of the question.

By 1908, the railroads were doing well again thanks to government freight and postal contracts. But Mary's health was failing. Mears elected to take his wife to a better climate and left Colorado for California.

Mears' Colorado railroads continued to be profitable but suffered from management from afar. In 1931, Mears' daughter, Cora Mears Pitcher, took over as president of her father's railroad empire. She was one of the first female railroad presidents in the country. Sadly, Otto Mears died later that year at age ninety-one.

Cora had always been involved in her father's railroad business and first owned stock as a young adult. Her husband, James Robertson Pitcher Jr., first rose to head her father's railroad company following Mears' move to California. But when she became president, Cora brought a newfound respectability to her father's company. She improved the rail cars and added Pullman cars and extra dining cars in an effort to attract tourists. Cora continued to run the Silverton Northern line to the San Juan mines until the outbreak of World War II, when many mines were shut down.

Cora Mears Pitcher was the first female president and the last president of the Silverton Northern Railroad. Following her death on September 8, 1948, at the age of sixty-nine, the railroad company was sold. Yet, during her tenure as president, Cora proudly carried on her father's legacy.

CREEDE

Bee McClure: A Modern Mining Woman

"The cliffs are solid silver with wondrous wealth untold
And the beds of running rivers are lined with glittering gold
While the world is filled with sorrows and hearts must break and bleed
It's day all day in the day-time
and there is no night in Creede"
—Cy Warman

The discovery of silver in 1889 in Willow Creek Canyon just north of what would eventually be the mining camp of Creede was the beginning of legendary riches. Before year end, the population had grown to 10,000 residents!

A century later, in January 1985, after producing over 25 million ounces of silver and 48 million pounds of lead, the Bulldog Mountain Mine closed due to the low price of silver. With mine production costs averaging $7 to $8 per ounce of silver and silver priced at $6 an ounce, it was simply not profitable to operate. Yet it had been a long and legendary run for the mine and the history of Creede.

Nicholas Creede struck pay dirt with his discovery and yelled out "Holy Moses, I've struck it rich!" And so he had. The Holy Moses Mine was the first of many for this region. Soon, the mining camp took the name of Creede and legends were born.

But that was just the beginning. Creede's second discovery was a silver vein laced with amethyst. He called it the Amethyst Mine. On Bulldog Mountain, a mile northwest of Creede, Doctor A. J. Biles discovered a rich vein of silver in 1894. He named his claim the "Bulldog" in honor of the mountain. The Bulldog vein ran close to the surface, yet it would be years before its true riches were known. When that happened, the Bulldog became the longest-operating mine in the Creede Mining District.

With the repeal of the Sherman Silver Purchase Act in 1893, the government no longer required silver as backing for the American dollar. Overnight, silver production ground to a halt. The Bulldog Mine managed a small mining crew to stay in business. But the mine began taking on water and Dr. Biles began digging a tunnel. He labored for three years, but when it was completed the 861-foot tunnel snaked through the heart of Bulldog Mountain, draining the mine.

Left: *Shown here in 1892, Creede was a bustling mining town built on the precious metals in its mountains.* *PHOTOGRAPH COURTESY OF THE LIBRARY OF CONGRESS, LC-USZ62-47751.*

Biles managed to procure valuable mining claims, sink more shafts, and develop the Bulldog Mine holdings. The Bulldog Mountain fault system proved to have an enormous amount of high-grade silver. A tunnel was built from north to south to access the Bulldog vein.

By the 1920s, A. J. Biles' holdings were absorbed into a new company, the Bulldog Leasing, Mining and Milling Company. The tunnel was extended more than 1,000 feet but no mineral ore was found. Soon after, the company ceased operation. The prospectus of the Bulldog Leasing, Mining and Milling Company held out hope, speculating that "our own Bulldog lode may yet prove to be the great undiscovered motherlode of Creede."

How prophetic this would turn out to be. In 1961, Bulldog Mountain, Inc. resumed operation of the mine. A survey from the U.S. Geological Survey noted that the Bulldog Mountain fault might intersect with the Amethyst vein. With the potential of undiscovered mineral ore, the company's prospectus did indeed prove correct. It would be the "motherlode of Creede."

That was about the time when Bee McClure went to work at the Bulldog Mountain Mine.

Bee was born during the Spanish Flu epidemic of 1918. She lived through it, and was tough, strong-willed, and sturdy because of it. Shortly after Bee's birth, her family moved to La Garita, Colorado, where her father managed the fish hatchery and her mother taught school. Eventually, Bee met and fell in love with a local boy by the name of Eugene. The two courted and married.

Following the Great Depression, the Bulldog Mountain Mine was bought by the Homestake Mining Company. Meanwhile, Bee's husband, Gene, opened a hardware store to supply the mines, which were all operating once again. Bee remembered:

> Ended up he [Gene] ran the whole hardware store, and it was big business in those mining days because all the mines would always buy their supplies there. Gosh, we'd haul truckloads of dynamite up that mountain. We had that railroad coming in to town too. When they'd get a carload of dynamite and supplies, it would make us all grand. Gosh, it just took a lot to get that boxcar unloaded. We had a powder magazine down by where the old dump ground used to be, down out of Creede about four or five miles. The powder magazine was where we kept our dynamite; and then a separate one where we kept the caps. We couldn't store them together. We didn't even deliver them together. But they were a big item around here.[9]

After Gene died in 1967, Bee ran the hardware store for a few years then sold it. Two days later she went to work for the Homestake Mining Company as the office manager.

> I worked up at the mine. I went to work for the Homestake Mining Company on the first day of July, 1967. I was the office manager. I liked it up there too. That's the reason I can live where I live now; good salary and good pension. Sometimes I had to go into the mine to check inventory. I didn't like it a bit. I was so glad to get out. When you'd see that light hole coming up—I was glad. But those guys, I don't know if they liked it, but I tell you there were some mighty good miners up there.

In January 1985, the Bulldog Mine finally shut down. With the mine closure, the last mine to do so in the Creede Mining District, the mining era was officially over. In more than ninety-four years, the Creede Mining District produced an estimated 85 million ounces of silver.

Today, Creede is a fine example of a tough mining town, and Bee McClure was a central mining figure in its later years. Bee McClure Drive in Creede was named in her memory, a fitting honor for the mining lady.

TELLURIDE

Harriet Fish Backus: Tomboy Bride

"The San Juans are the wildest and most desolate mountains in all of Colorado."
—H. H. Bancroft

Harriet Anna Fish grew up in Oakland, California, during the mid-1800s. She was trained to be a teacher as so many young women were. Then, at the age of twenty-two, in 1908, Harriet married her high school sweetheart, George Backus.

George was a mining engineer working at the mines high in the San Juan Mountains. The marriage was an adventure in itself—one that set off a series of adventures for young Harriet. She later wrote, "Working for the Telegraph Company after the San Francisco earthquake, preceded by two years of teaching school, had not conditioned me for 'wild adventuring.' But since George could not leave a new position for a trip to California, I must go to him."[10]

After a grueling train trip from California to Denver, in sub-zero weather and arriving a day late, Harriet finally was reunited with her sweetheart. "At one in the morning I stepped off the train for George's eager greeting," she wrote. "Together at last. Next morning he hurried to the jeweler to have the date corrected in the wedding ring. Meanwhile, I spent the time laying out my wedding clothes."

Later that same day they were married. She recalled:

> In the manse of one of Denver's splendid churches, George placed on my finger the wide gold band which never has been taken off, and Dr. Coyle said, "I now pronounce you man and wife."
>
> On Saturday night we left Denver, arriving the following morning in Salida where we changed to a narrow-gauge railway. George dashed to a store and returned with a can of sardines and some stale soda crackers for our honeymoon breakfast. The Stub, a small dingy train, was to carry us to Telluride and proved to be a foretaste of what was ahead.

When Harriet arrived in Telluride, she found the area a bit alien. It was situated at a very high altitude, more than two miles above sea level, unlike her previous home, which lay at sea level.

The trip to the mines above Telluride was more of an expedition. George had bought Harriet extra petticoats, tights, and wool dresses, and swaddled her in shawls and even a fur wrap. The path up the mountain was narrow and winding, hugging the mountainside, with sheer cliffs on the other side. "So high were the walls on the three sides of the valley and so narrow the floor between that in winter the sunlight reached the little town only a few hours of the day," Harriet wrote. "By mid-afternoon the purple shadows of cliffs dropped a pall over the rugged settlement."

Avalanches could crash down and bury people in an instant. Harriet described being trapped on the trail because of an avalanche ahead of them They had to wait until miners came down and could clear the path from the opposite direction. Also, Harriet was irritated by a constant loud thumping noise. "That's the voice of sixty stamps in the Tomboy Mill," George explained. "And it's a noise mining people like to hear. It never stops unless there is trouble."

The first home she had was made of raw lumber. She used newspapers to cover the cracks in the walls and keep the snow and the wind out. It helped—a little. The wind would howl and the house, perched on the mountainside, would actually rock. After a snowstorm, Harriet would have to sweep the snow from the wooden floor.

After one particular storm, George spent the entire day digging out a path to the outhouse 100 yards from the house.

Because George was a mining engineer, he and Harriet were better off economically than most of the miners. That is not to say that Harriet did not suffer privations and hardships living in a mining camp.

Harriet eventually learned to cook at such a high altitude. But there were challenges. She had to plan her meals very carefully. Food and supplies were either delivered by mule train once a month or George had to make the long and treacherous trip to Telluride for goods.

Harriet made quite a few friends, both male and female. She wasn't nearly as lonely as she thought she would be. Then, in early March, George lost his job. At Harriet's urging, George applied for a job at the famed Tomboy Mine, nearly 12,000 feet above above sea level. It was also the richest mine in the Savage Basin of the San Juans.

Harriet and George moved to a new home "on a bench above the tailings." Harriet wrote:

> The view was superb. On three sides the great white range of mountains stood close like a surrounding guard of honor and we could look down the deep canyon as it sloped off into the valleys toward the horizon.
>
> Our entrance porch was made of three rotting planks weakly supported by a six-inch thick log on the down side. Squatted flat on the ground unpainted, like all the other shacks, it measured twenty-two feet by ten feet in size and was built of one-inch boards with barrens, but no lining whatever. The only day light came through the doorways.
>
> Except for two houses at the upper workings, our shack was the highest. I could see the panorama below, miners walking the pipe lines, riderless horses returning to the stables, occasional skiers catapulting down the opposite peak, packtrains on their wearying journeys—fascinating scenes indelibly etched on my memory.

Horses were the mode of transportation in these mountains and Harriet grew to love them. Her favorite horse was Old Chief. She exclaimed, "How I loved them! Never did I lose the pleasure of knowing that with an affectionate pat I could dismiss my horse confident that he would return to his barn with the certainty of a homing pigeon. And how my temper blazed when I saw a horse slowly approaching the end of the trail, head drooping low, flanks dripping foam, for I knew what it meant—a miner in a hurry!" In time, Harriet learned to master the rigid, cold life high in the San Juan Mountains. She even came to enjoy it. She wrote, "We didn't miss the so-called luxuries of a city. We were together and oh, so happy! And the days flew by." In one memorable scene, George and Harriet rode their horses high above to Virginia Pass:

> Standing more than two-and-a-half miles above the line where sky and oceans meet we could see our little settlement, diminished by distance. Shacks, boardinghouse, and mill dotted the depths of that white-crested spur of the range curving like a sickle above them, the first sparse sprinkling of trees increasing in density down the slopes.
>
> We could see what Bancroft meant by "mountains beyond mountains." On the northeast slope of the Sneffles range in Imogene Basin was located the famous Camp Bird mine and Mill with outlet, the town of Ouray, hidden like Telluride in the narrow canyon below.

Perched at timberline, the Tomboy Mine was a tough environment for miners, let alone for raising a family.
PHOTOGRAPH COURTESY OF DENVER PUBLIC LIBRARY, SPECIAL COLLECTIONS.

Harriet Fish Backus thrived on life in the mountains at the Tomboy Mine near Telluride. PHOTOGRAPH COURTESY OF THE TELLURIDE HISTORICAL MUSEUM.

Indeed, as Harriet wrote, time did pass much too quickly. She noted, "Summer passed all too quickly. The solitude of our mountain cabin, the splendor of azure skies kissing mountain peaks, the vista of winding roads clinging to precipices, far away valleys disappearing into the distance, all mingled in nature's harmony, lulled me into daytime reveries—the wonders of this paradise of magnificence and dreams of happy years ahead."

Harriet soon learned how dangerous it could be to care for a baby at Tomboy Mine's high altitude. She relied on fellow miners' wives to give advice and help her in stressful times with no doctor for miles. Harriet wrote of a scary time:

> The baby had colic every afternoon and Letta Tuller came after school to help me. Following the colic came a disagreeable experience with pinkeye. How did Harriet get that? How in this isolated spot with its rarified, cold, purified air, so fatal to insects, did the germs of whooping cough and meningitis exist and strike in winter? Next, I caught the infection from the baby and had pinkeye too.

In the spring of 1910, George got a mining job far away from the San Juan Mountains, which Harriet had come to love.

> The winter of 1909 to 1910 piled up an average of eight to ten feet of snow throughout Savage Basin. It was a rugged place to live although we had been happy and certainly never bored by monotony. Being together was all we needed.
>
> We had achieved more than our goal, dear friends, wild adventures, our precious child, and George's valuable experience in varied phases of mining and milling procedures.

In her memoir of her time in the San Juans, *Tomboy Bride,* Harriet wrote, "We enjoyed traveling by automobile, steamliners, luxurious ocean liners, and airplanes. But the old creaking wagons, the sliding sleds, and the back of Old Chief are among the most cherished memories of the woman who long ago had been a Tomboy Bride."

Notes

1. McLean, Evalyn Walsh. *Father Struck It Rich.* Little, Brown, and Company, 1936. p. 54. All quotes attributed to Evalyn Walsh McLean come from this book, her memoir.
2. Stewart, John. *Thomas F. Walsh: Progressive Businessman and Colorado Mining Tycoon.* University Press of Colorado, 2012. p. 80.
3. McLean, *Father Struck It Rich,* p. 201.
4. *Washington Post,* September 29, 1997.
5. ibid.
6. Crum, Josie Moore. *Rails Among the Peaks.* Railroader Printing House, 1956. p. 9.
7. Beebe, Lucius, and Charles Clegg. *Narrow Gauge in the Rockies.* Heimburger House Publishing, 1993. p. 102.
8. The *San Juan Democrat,* June 1889.
9. All quotes from Bee McClure are from an interview found in *Women of the Upper Rio Grande: Beartown to Creede: Memories from 1920 through 1960,* Donning Company Publishers, 2011, by Laura McClenny.
10. Backus, Harriet Fish. *Tomboy Bride.* Pruett Press, 1969. p. 3. All quotes from Harriet are from this book, her memoir.

6

THE GREATEST GOLD CAMP ON EARTH

In a Cripple Creek mine circa 1897, a woman holds a candle while men stand poised with hammers and drills. PHOTOGRAPH BY EDGAR A. YELTON, COURTESY OF PIKES PEAK DISTRICT LIBRARY.

ON THE SOUTH SIDE OF PIKES PEAK lies the legendary mountain mining district of Cripple Creek. Men have passed through the region for centuries: Spanish explorers, French and American trappers and traders, pathfinders, homesteaders and ranchers, and finally those eager men frantically searching for that ever-elusive gold strike. One such man was Bob Womack, who struck the first paying gold strike, and Cripple Creek was born.

But what of the women? Yes, they were here too. We just don't often hear of them. Women like Emma Langdon, a linotypist who went to work covering the labor strikes in Victor, and Katy Bemore, a witness to the violence of the strikes.

Or Mollie Katherine Gortner, who literally sat on a gold mine; Mollie O'Bryan, who was the first woman to serve on the Mining Stock Exchange; and Julia Skolas, who captured mining life with her camera. And then there was Ethel Frizzell Carlton, who continued her husband's labor activist work into the twentieth century.

Hard work, family, and community mattered to them. They were strong and they were resilient. These women contributed to the story of gold in Cripple Creek every bit as much as their male counterparts. It's about time we knew their stories.

CRIPPLE CREEK

Mary Katherine Gortner: Sitting on a Gold Mine

Like many, the Gortner family came west for adventure, health, and wealth. Originally from Ottumwa, Iowa, the Gortner family—Henry, Mary (who preferred the name Mollie), and their two children, Perry and Elizabeth—first settled on North Nevada Street in Colorado Springs. It was here in the spring of 1891 that they heard news of a rich gold strike at the south base of Pikes Peak.

A wandering cowpoke, Bob Womack, had been searching the creeks of an overgrown cow pasture for gold for years. And he found it—a couple of times. But no one paid attention to Ol' Bob; they'd heard the stories before. It was October 20, 1890, when Womack filed the El Paso claim. Six months later, in April 1891, the Cripple Creek Mining District was formed.

Mollie's son, Perry, was among the surveyors during a trip to the district. Their goal was to map the many mining claims of the area. Perry's stories of rich gold finds were astonishing and his enthusiasm was contagious. Soon, Mollie was packing the family buckboard with picks and shovels and various supplies. In due time Mollie took her wagon south to Cripple Creek.

Arriving in Cripple Creek, Mollie stayed with her son in his crude home, part log, part canvas tent. On a clear, crisp September day, Mollie ventured up Poverty Gulch to catch a glimpse of an elk herd her son had told her about. She knew the area well. Just a few days prior to this, Mollie had made her way up the gulch to Womack's El Paso Mine. One this day, as she made her way up, she passed the El Paso, and approximately 300 yards higher, she sat down to rest. Looking about, Mollie's eye fixed on a curious rock formation. In the bright sunlight, it seemed to wink at her. She picked up a few pieces of the rock specimens and shoved them into her dress pockets.

When the specimens assayed at $250 to the ton, Mollie knew she had found her gold mine. Mollie staked her claim and called it the Mollie Kathleen Mine. It is said that the men at the claim office were reluctant in granting Mollie the claim. In doing so, she became the first woman mine owner in the Cripple Creek District. Mollie enlisted her son, Perry, to run the day-to-day operations while Mollie provided the pluck with her ingenuity. It was not long before the main shaft had reached the 1,000-foot level, which was a marvel at the time. A miner's superstition held that women were unlucky in mines. For this reason, the miners vacated the mine whenever Mollie was on the premises.

Mollie Gortner was the first woman mine owner in the Cripple Creek District. PHOTOGRAPH COURTESY OF BRIAN LEVINE.

For the next twenty-five years, Mollie's mine produced a good, steady supply of gold ore. This was no small feat for a woman-owned mine against her male counterparts or the mining corporations formed after 1900. Although the Mollie Kathleen Mine was never a top-ten producer for the district, it provided a nice income for the Gortner family, producing an average of $200,000 annually.

Mary "Mollie" Kathleen Gortner died in 1917. Her husband, Henry, died the following year. Both are buried in the Evergreen Cemetery in Colorado Springs. Perry received one-third interest in the mine and continued to manage it until his death in 1949.

During World War I, to help with operating expenses, a portion of the mine was opened to tourists. With no head protection, visitors clamored to ride open buckets down the 1,000-foot shaft. As it was still an operating mine, miners took turns guiding the tourists underground by candlelight. So high was visitor volume that changes were quickly made in the mining operating schedule. Tours were conducted during the daytime hours and mining work was done at night. Thus, the Mollie Kathleen Mine conducted business on two fronts. This was conducive for what business was to become in Cripple Creek.

When the Carlton Mill closed in 1961, the processing of ore ended for a time. Many working mines, including the Mollie Kathleen, were forced to shut down. But this great mine, discovered and owned by a woman, would produce again.

More than 100 years following the Pikes Peak Gold Rush, Cripple Creek was enjoying a new rush to the mountains—tourists. While the Mollie Kathleen Mine was forced to halt ore production in 1961, the tourist operations continued. Touring by the day and mining by night seemed to be a winning combination for all involved.

As the oldest continuously operating mine in the Cripple Creek District, the Mollie Kathleen saw many improvements during the 1960s. A shiny steel headframe replaced the old lumbered frame. A new hoist house was built with new equipment inside. And on the tourist side of the business, new mining displays were constructed at the seventh and tenth levels. Today, the Mollie Kathleen Mine is the only mine open to tourists that features a 1,000-foot shaft.

Then, in the mid-1970s, it happened again—gold! A blasting crew uncovered a body of ore, which assayed at 1.5 troy ounces of gold to the ton. While the new discovery created excitement around the world, there was still no practical or economic way to process the gold ore. However, the discovery of the ore led to new exploration, new tunnels, and another 1,000 feet were dug. Meanwhile the newly discovered body of ore glistened and sparkled under new underground electric lighting for the glory of the visitors.

Today, the Mollie Kathleen Mine hosts visitors from around the world. Two elevators take the tourists down 1,000 feet to the cold, dank, damp underground mine where trains roar through tunnels carrying their precious cargo—gold!

Mollie O'Bryan: Mining Her Business

Determined, ambitious, and strong spirited. That describes Mollie O'Bryan, the first woman to hold a seat on the board of the powerful Cripple Creek Mining Stock Exchange.

The young Irish lass by the name of Mollie was born to William and Mary O'Bryan on July 19, 1873. The second of two daughters, she was named Mary after her mother. Possibly to distinguish between herself and her mother, she was called "Mollie." The O'Bryan family came west from Missouri, settling in Lake City by the mid-1880s. William quickly found work among the many mines there. Following her schooling, Mollie obtained employment as a secretary in Lake City. During this time, Mollie gained a keen interest in the financial side of the mining business. She took positions with mining and brokerage firms to learn their intricate operations.

When gold was discovered in Cripple Creek in 1891, Mollie made big plans to be in the center of the action. In 1893, Mollie finally made her move. Arriving in Cripple Creek, she immediately found work as a stenographer on the west side of Second Street. The location was ideally situated within a short walking distance to the Cripple Creek Mining Stock Exchange building on Bennett Avenue.

Mollie O'Bryan succeeded in mining due to her keen business sense and financial acumen. PHOTOGRAPH IN THE PUBLIC DOMAIN.

The repeal of the Sherman Silver Purchase Act in 1893 caused silver stock prices to plummet on the stock exchange while gold became quite lucrative. And Mollie knew just how to increase her chances at wealth. Mollie began investing in several mines in the Cripple Creek Mining District. At $5 blocks, she soon had built up an impressive portfolio. When the various stocks reached a certain price, Mollie would sell off and reinvest her profits. In this manner, Mollie was able to afford the $5,000 security bond as well as the $400 membership fee required to belong to the brokers association.[1]

At an average stock price of four cents, Mollie continued buying and selling mining stock at record profits.[2] She soon caught the eye of Charles N. Miller, a stock broker who had experienced only moderate success. Miller soon discovered the secret to Mollie's success. Continuing her contract work as a stenographer, Mollie was able to gain inside knowledge on the business dealings of mining throughout the district. Obtaining such inside information was a legitimate way of doing business at the time. Following the stock market crash of 1929, the Securities and Exchange Commission was formed in 1934, which disallowed such practices.

During 1894 and 1895, Mollie bought mining properties all over the district, including the Blue Chime claim in Poverty Gulch, the Little Diamond Mine on Battle Mountain, and the Lonely Mine on Bull Hill. Then she and Charles Miller, along with T. B. Burbridge, B. F. N. Macrorie, and A. G. Young, formed the Big Four Investment Company.[3]

So successful was the Big Four that Mollie gained a favorable reputation from Cripple Creek to Colorado Springs. The firm soon became a leader in the Cripple Creek Mining Stock Exchange, with an average yearly business revenue of $3 million dollars.

Due to her success and business acumen, Mollie was elected to join the board of the Cripple Creek Mining Stock Exchange in 1896.[4] She became the first woman to hold a seat on the board. Nevertheless, Mollie continued with her stenography work, moving to an office in the Tutt and Penrose Block on Bennett Avenue. This was conveniently close to the new National Hotel, the social hub of Cripple Creek.

In 1899, Mollie bought the Teutonic Mine for $3,500. A month later, she was offered $35,000 for the mine. She declined the offer. A few years later, Mollie formed the Consolidated Gold Mine Company along with partners Charles Miller, A. G. Young, H. E. Hoyt, and Mollie's brother-in-law, Zeno Felder, a Cripple Creek dentist. Through this company, shares of various mines were bought and sold with an average price per share of seven and a half cents.[5]

In 1903, due to a looming labor strike, the Consolidated Gold Mine Company lived up to its name by consolidating several of its mines, including the Juanita and New Century Mines. This allowed for better management during the labor strike that was to come.

Mollie now turned her attention back to the Teutonic Mine on Gold Hill, which connected with her Damon Mine. By 1906, the main shaft would reach a depth of 200 feet where several rich veins were discovered.

In 1904, the looming labor strike finally happened. The most violent labor war in Cripple Creek history left scars on the hills. It paralyzed gold production, and many of the smaller mines went bankrupt. In an effort to remain solvent, Mollie began selling off some of her mines, little by little.

As mining operations were becoming more expensive and with smaller returns or profit, by 1909, Mollie was left with only the Teutonic Mine in her portfolio. It was about this time that Mollie and Charles Miller dissolved their partnership. Cashing out of Cripple Creek, Miller left for San Francisco where he opened another brokerage company.

Unlike Miller, Mollie believed in Cripple Creek. She remained in the district, working as a mining broker and continuing in her stenography role. In later years, she lived with her sister Ida and brother-in-law, Zeno Felder, at 140 West Golden.[6]

Mollie O'Bryan was the first woman to hold a seat on the Cripple Creek Mining Stock Exchange, shown here circa 1895. PHOTOGRAPH BY HORACE S. POLEY, COURTESY OF DENVER PUBLIC LIBRARY, SPECIAL COLLECTIONS.

Mollie O'Bryan died in this home of a cerebral hemorrhage on December 30, 1922. She was only forty-nine years old. Mollie was buried in the Mount Pisgah cemetery.

Mollie O'Bryan worked in a man's world but made it on her own. She achieved great accomplishments, including a seat on the board of the Cripple Creek Stock Mining Exchange.

Julia Skolas: Cripple Creek in Pictures

Julia Skolas is one of the very few female photographers in the nineteenth century. Described in James Semple's *Representative Woman of Colorado* as a very successful artistic photographer, her work is admired even today.

Julia was born on the family farm on May 14, 1863, to Norwegian parents, Aslak and Aasne Skolas, near Cottage Grove, Wisconsin, just east of Madison. The eighth of nine children, from an early age Julia learned to be independent, strong-headed, and determined. Julia came west alone at the age of twenty-seven in 1890. She first settled in Denver where she found work at a local photography studio in downtown Denver at 1624 Curtis Street. There, under the tutelage of Charles A. Nast, Julia learned the art of photography. Nast made a portrait image of Julia at his studio in 1893.

After accomplishments in her new trade, Julia moved to Colorado Springs in 1896. Here she opened her own studio, which she ran successfully for nearly a decade. Julia was a member of several business and social groups, including the Progress Club and labor organizations, and was a founding member of the Colorado Springs Badger Club, a group numbering ninety-one, with ties to Wisconsin. The June 28, 1903, edition of the *Colorado Springs Gazette* mentioned Julia in a feature on the club, reporting, "At the annual Badger Club meeting, Miss Skolas presented each guest with their name on a puzzle, which proved to be a little sketch illustrating a colored photograph of North Cheyenne Cañon."

An accomplished photographer, Julia Skolas made this self-portrait in 1910. PHOTOGRAPH BY JULIA SKOLAS, COURTESY OF PIKES PEAK LIBRARY DISTRICT.

In 1907, Julia took on a labor of love. She moved to Cripple Creek for the sole purpose of photographing the interior and exterior of the mines of the district. She set up her photography studio on Bennett Avenue, the town's main thoroughfare. In 1910, to capitalize on the new fad of souvenir postcards, Julia began selling photo postcards.

Julia remained in Cripple Creek until 1920. When she left, for some reason she left behind many of her glass plate negatives. After a short visit to her native state of Wisconsin, Julia returned to Colorado, again taking up residence in Denver by 1924. Perhaps the reason for leaving behind her glass plate negatives was that she was gradually giving up photography, as this advertisement in the *Denver Post* issue of January 18, 1925, indicates: "ONE 8x10 view camera, ONE 8x10 portrait lens, cheap. Skolas, Apt. 29 1/2 1720 Logan."

Remaining in Denver, Julia, now well into her sixties, found work as a candle maker, a milliner, and even a candy saleswoman. In 1931 Julia returned to Wisconsin where she found a home in Madison. There, she died of a heart attack on December 31, 1934.

Julia Skolas left behind an impressive body of work including studio portraits, landscapes, and mining images that capture the heart of Cripple Creek.

Ethel Frizzell Carlton: A Female Force in Mining

When Ethel Frizzell married Cripple Creek's wealthiest business tycoon, she also avoided a terrible romantic scandal, at least by Cripple Creek standards.

Ethel Irene Frizzell was born on October 1, 1877, in St. Paul, Minnesota.[7] The daughter of Alonzo and Mary Catherine Frizzell, she moved with her family to Vermont at a young age. Following the news of the gold discovery at Cripple Creek in 1891, Alonzo, a well-respected property attorney, moved his family to Colorado and then settled in Colorado Springs, where he began buying mining properties in the Cripple Creek Mining District. Through his business, the Frizzells became friends with several well-respected families such as the Charles Howberts, the Harry Blackmers, and Alexander and Mrs. Hunt.

In 1896, the Howberts invited the Frizzells and their eighteen-year-old daughter, Ethel, to the grand opening gala of Cripple Creek's newest hostelry, the National Hotel. Ethel must have been thrilled to be attending her first ball in Colorado where she could meet all the eligible young men. But the young debutante had a problem. Her dance card was soon filled up by one man. His name was Albert "Bert" Eugene Carlton. The *Cripple Creek Morning Times* carried the story the following day:

> Such a scene as was enacted last night at the National Hotel might have been witnessed in any eastern metropolis garnished with wealth and polished with age. That it could have taken place in a supposedly crude, uncultured mining camp in the West was, in this reporter's opinion, a matter of pride. The cream of Cripple Creek society was present. The exquisite gowns of the ladies were accentuated by the somber black swallow-tails of the gentlemen. Perfect taste prevailed in the minutest details. It would have been difficult to find a single costume that would not have passed muster in any exclusive ballroom in the East. Altogether, the affair reflected distinction on Cripple Creek's elite. Among the fashionable dancers were Miss Claribel Levens, radiant in a toilette of cream lace garnitured with pink ribbons; Miss Ethel Frizzell, strikingly beautiful in turquoise blue chiffon.

Bert was one of Cripple Creek's most influential business entrepreneurs and was well on his way to becoming known as the "King of Cripple Creek." On that night, he had set his sights on Ethel. Ethel's problem? Bert was eleven years her senior. Mrs. Howbert wasted no time in fixing Ethel's problem by telling Ethel and her parents that Bert was already engaged.

Ethel Frizzell's looks turned heads, but it was her financial savvy and social advocacy that earned her a successful and rewarding life. PHOTOGRAPH COURTESY OF PIKES PEAK LIBRARY DISTRICT.

Ethel stayed away from Bert Carlton as much as possible. It became more difficult, however, after the Frizzells moved to Cripple Creek where Alonzo opened his law practice on Bennett Avenue.[8] Then, what Ethel had been avoiding happened—scandal.

A certain Mrs. Eva Stanton Carlton had arrived in Cripple Creek looking for her husband—

Bert Carlton. The gossip blew like the mountain wind. Soon it became a statewide sensation when the Colorado Springs and Denver newspapers picked up the story—Bert had both a wife and fiancée. Ethel's inclination to stay away from Bert Carlton had been a wise one.

Before the year was out, Bert had managed to set up his fiancée in Colorado Springs with a large boarding house, all the new rage in business. He then obtained a quick divorce, with the help of friend and lawyer Henry Blackmer, by paying off the wife. All the while Bert was sending love notes to Ethel.

After a respectable amount of time had passed—two years—Ethel Irene Frizzell married Albert Eugene Carlton on December 1, 1901, in Washington, D.C.[9] Following a honeymoon in New York City, the newlyweds returned to Cripple Creek where they were received at the National Hotel and a party was given in their honor.

Mr. and Mrs. Carlton settled in at Bert's lavish apartment above his First National Bank at 347 Bennett Avenue. While Bert jumped right back into his various businesses, Ethel, too, wasted no time in volunteering herself for charitable causes. One story has it that Ethel was clearing out her closet of old ball gowns when her maid asked if the gowns could be donated to charity, and just like that, a charitable cause was born.

Soon, Ethel became Cripple Creek's social leader and benefactor. She helped finance the arts and led in humanitarian causes as well as social reform. Women relished the chance to dress up in all their finery and attend a social function hosted by Ethel Carlton.

Along with their many business interests, the Carltons controlled several mines in the district. With their wealth, Bert expanded his First National Bank and invested in many enterprises, including railroads and the Holly Sugar Corporation, when mining slowed due to underground floods. Bert saw a solution to that problem, and in 1908 took ownership of the Roosevelt Drainage Tunnel when that company fell into financial difficulty. Under his leadership and ingenuity, many mines were saved and mining improved in the district. In 1910, Bert made Ethel his business partner when the couple established the Golden Cycle Corporation.

The mining business in Cripple Creek changed following the violent and bloody labor war of 1904. Mine owners either consolidated or sold out to large corporations. But Bert Carlton saw this coming. There was nobody better at sensing mining changes than Bert. The couple's Golden Cycle Corporation soon began buying up smaller mines until the corporation had a controlling interest in the mining district. With such control, the Carltons were able to dictate the assay value of ore and, through the bank, set interest rates, lease options, and act as a leader in wage control and hours of operation.

Then, in 1915, the Carltons gained controlling interest in John T. Milliken's Golden Cycle Mine at Victor and the Golden Cycle Mill in Colorado City. The $4 million deal now meant the Carltons controlled every aspect of Cripple Creek mining. When the Carltons bought into the Cresson, the richest mine in the district, for another $4 million, the mining monopoly was sealed. Bert became president of the Cresson Mine, and his mining partners—his brother Leslie, Spencer Penrose, Adolph Zang, and Claude Boettcher of Denver—all had seats on the board. In 1922, Bert bought the Vindicator Mine. With this purchase, the Carltons now owned all the large producing mines in the district; only the Portland and Strong Mines escaped their control.

With such control came wealth beyond belief. Bert and Ethel moved to Colorado Springs where they bought a house on Wood Avenue (Millionaires Row.) Ethel wasted no time in setting up her charities and jumped right into her philanthropic work. Her first act was to have a bandstand built at Monument Valley Park. She became an active supporter of the Colorado Springs Symphony, the Cheyenne Mountain Country Club, and the Garden of the Gods Club. Ethel would later become a member of the Broadmoor Golf Club and even the Denver Country Club. She was also an avid supporter of the Central City Opera.

Closer to home, Ethel enjoyed entertaining her friends and associates with lavish lobster dinners. Crates of champagne were brought in for consumption by all.

Meanwhile, Bert and Ethel continued to grow their controlling interests in Cripple Creek. Bert had sold the business that got him started years ago, the Colorado Transfer and Trade Company, in 1898, to buy the First National Bank. Now, in 1915, he bought it back. And by purchasing Henry Blackmer's shares of the Midland Terminal Railroad stock, the Carltons now had a controlling interest in the railroad industry. But they weren't done. In 1922, they bought out their partners in the Vindicator Mine. In essence, Bert and Ethel now owned nearly all of the businesses in Cripple Creek.

But mountain mining wasn't their only interest. In 1910, they had partnered with friends, Spencer and Julia Penrose, to invest in several enterprises. In 1916, Bert had bought stock in the Broadmoor Hotel, built by his friend, Spec Penrose. Years later, in 1929, the Carltons bought a suite at the hotel and moved in while their new home was being built in Pine Valley, north of Colorado Springs. Ethel Carlton and Julie Penrose ran the Broadmoor Sport Shop together for years. But Bert and Ethel enjoyed their new home for only a short time. Sadly, on September 7, 1931, Albert Eugene Carlton died of uremic poisoning. He was sixty-five years old.

In the summer of 1934, a grieving Ethel accepted the invitation of Julie and Spec Penrose to stay with them in their new estate near Honolulu, Hawaii. In a letter to his granddaughter, Pauline, Spec wrote, "We are becoming more and more delighted with the place. Yesterday we were down at the boat to meet Mrs. Carlton and Mrs. Wilcox of Denver."[10]

Following Bert's death in 1931, Ethel took over management of the vast Carlton empire, a total net worth of $227 million. Under Ethel's control, the Carlton Tunnel was dug deeper, through six miles of granite, to drain the Cripple Creek District mines. This was achieved just below the 7,000-foot level. But both world wars caused a labor shortage, and demand for gold ore fell off. A cyanide mill could treat the precious metal at a cost of $3 per ton. At a cost of $2 million to build, Ethel felt it would help the miners and the Cripple Creek economy. Thus, the mill was built and brought mining back in Cripple Creek.

After Spencer Penrose died in December 1939, Julie and Ethel traveled the world together as often as they could.

In 1954, Congress appropriated funds for the construction of the U.S. Air Force Academy near Colorado Springs. The land selected included Ethel Carlton's home in Pine Valley. After selling her property to the government, Ethel took up permanent residence at the Broadmoor Hotel.

Ethel Carlton remained active in her philanthropic work, as well as in politics and social events. All the while she kept her hand in the operations of the various Carlton holdings.

Ethel Irene Frizzell Carlton died on December 14, 1958, at the age of eighty-one. She had been recuperating from a knee infection at Glockner-Penrose Hospital in Colorado Springs when she suddenly had a heart attack.[11]

The legacy of the grand dame of Cripple Creek still lives in the many mining projects in and around the district.

VICTOR

The mines in and around Victor were the source of most of the gold in the Cripple Creek Mining District. One of the richest, the Gold Coin Mine, was located right in the heart of the mining town. Thus, the town was dubbed the "City of Mines."

Victor and its mines were the source of considerable activity. From the hustle and bustle of mining production to the hum of machinery, Victor was a busy place.

With a monthly payroll of just under $1 million, Victor was fast outpacing its rival, Cripple Creek.

At its peak in 1900, the Victor mines produced more than $500 million dollars in gold.

Today, Victor has maintained its Victorian mountain charm. A few of the mines can still be seen up on Battle Mountain, the site of so much mining history and lore that began over a century ago.

Emma Florence Langdon: A Voice for the Miners

Emma Langdon had no interest in the women's rights movement of the early twentieth century. Gender issues didn't concern her. What concerned Emma was equal pay for equal work. When the labor strike of 1903–1904 broke out in the Cripple Creek Mining District, she took an active role despite, or because of, her gender.

Emma Florence Parker was born on September 29, 1875, on the Tennessee farm of her parents. In 1890, at the age of fifteen, Emma married J. W. Lockett. Three years later, a daughter, Lucile was born, their only child. Her marriage did not last and two years later she married Charles G. Langdon. A printer by trade, Langdon moved his new family to his hometown of Junction City, Kansas, for better employment opportunities.

In 1903, Emma and her husband moved to the Cripple Creek Mining District and joined the staff of the *Victor Daily Record,* one of eight newspapers in the district. While Langdon initially worked as a typesetter, Emma became an apprentice linotype operator.

This was a time of growing tension between mine owners and miners. The owners resisted the labor unions, principally the Western Federation of Miners (WFM). Once the WFM had a firm hold in the district, the situation grew worse. The labor union fought for wages of $3.45 a day and an eight-hour workday. The mine owners refused, as the current wage of $3.00 a day was above average compared to many Colorado mines, a wage that had been set following the labor strike of 1894.[12] The mine owners held a united front and formed the Mine Owners Association (MOA).

As tensions mounted, armed guards were placed at many mines. With their demands unmet, the miners finally went on strike on March 17, 1903. As days turned into weeks, the mine owners hired replacement workers, called scabs, to fill the vacated jobs of some 1,100 men. This naturally infuriated the labor union. When the strike began to take a violent turn, the MOA demanded the state take action.

Governor James Peabody sent in the state militia to squelch the strike. This only made matters worse.

The militia lined up miners on the streets of Victor and searched them for weapons or any incriminating evidence. Then a sheriff's deputy was shot. The state militia set up cannons on both sides of the street. Tensions were high.

Meanwhile, the *Victor Daily Record,* the only pro-union paper in the district, continued to cover the events and issues of the strike. When the paper erroneously claimed that one of the soldiers was an ex-convict, Adjutant General Sherman Bell ordered a raid on the offices of the *Victor Daily Record.* Bell, it seems, did not like the negative publicity or the pro-union stance of the paper.

On the night of September 29, 1903, soldiers raided and arrested the staff on duty at the *Victor Daily Record* offices. They took the workers, including editor George Kyner and Charles Langdon, to the jail at Goldfield, at the foot of Battle Mountain, known as the "bullpen."

Emma Langdon received a phone call alerting her to the arrest. She wasted no time in hurrying to the newspaper office. Under cover of darkness, Emma managed to sneak in. She then barricaded the doors and spent the night writing and typesetting the paper herself. By morning her work was done and the four-page edition was complete. She took a stack of papers and delivered them to those under arrest at the bullpen. Under the headline "Slightly Disfigured But Still in the Ring," Emma wrote:

> Tuesday night Sept. 29, 1903, at 11:05, the busiest hour on a morning paper, the Victor Daily Record, which had espoused the cause of the striking miners, was raided by the militia, and the entire force at work was "captured." The linotypes were humming, "catching the elevator" on every line, the foreman was fuming and "rushing" proofs, for "first side down" and "forms" must go to press at 11:30. Suddenly the door of the composing room flew open and in stalked Tom McCleelland with the air of a "conquering hero," followed by a file of yapping yokels dressed in garb of soldiers and armed to the teeth. "Halt!" yelled the fierce Tom. "Ground arms!" "Fix bayonets!" "Guard the entrances!"

The Cripple Creek Mining District was not under martial law, and therefore General Sherman Bell had no legal right to arrest the newspaper workers let alone hold them in jail. The men were soon released. In her 1908 book, *Labor's Greatest Conflict,* Emma recounted the scene somewhat dramatically:

> These employees were marched unceremoniously to the bull pen. Armed thugs forced them into a filthy and squalid little tent, absolutely barren of furniture or bedding, where they were told to stay or have their heads blown off if they appeared an inch outside of the entrance.

Emma used the newspaper coverage of the strike as the core of the book she would later publish on the subject. She worked on it alone until the early morning hours day after day. Eventually, *The Cripple Creek Strike,* a 248-page book, was self-published, typset, and bound at the *Victor Daily Record* offices. The book first appeared in March 1904, a full three months before the strike came to a violent end.

Emma Langdon's book, The Cripple Creek Strike, *won her nationwide recognition as an advocate for labor reforms and miners' rights.* PHOTOGRAPH FROM THE CRIPPLE CREEK STRIKE, *1905, COURTESY OF PIKES PEAK LIBRARY DISTRICT.*

Emma strongly condemned the mine owners and their allies. As Cripple Creek historian Brian Levine observed, "Langdon vehemently condemned the actions of the Mine Owners Association, Governor Peabody, and the Colorado State militia. At the same time, she praised the leaders of the Western Federation of Miners, Winfield Stratton and James Burns."

Emma's book was widely endorsed by members and officers of the Colorado Western Federation of Miners. It must be noted that this was before the strike ended in violence at the hands of Charles Moyer, president, and William "Big Bill" Haywood, secretary treasurer of the WFM. Nevertheless, in March 1904, Emma Langdon was a hero. She received hundreds of letters from across the country in support of her actions. The WFM presented her with a medal for her bravery and she became an honorary member. Emma would later become the publicist for the organization.

Emma's firsthand account, while credible, is very emotional, filled with hyperbole and a flair for dramatic effect. It is a mixture of advocacy supported by contemporary history and eyewitness accounts. Still, a Denver printer bought the rights and Emma expanded the volume in 1905 and again in 1908.

The strike came to a violent end when, on January 26, 1904, as the scab miners were coming off the night shift at W. S. Stratton's Independence Mine, the miner's cage was cut. The cage fell through the shaft and fifteen men died. The WFM accused the mine owner, Stratton, of neglecting safety standards. Mine officials accused union members of maliciously tampering with the machinery. Following this incident, 168 scab workers quit the Independence Mine.[13] The union won this round. The MOA, led by Stratton, James Doyle, and Jimmie Burns, retaliated by getting Albert Carlton to halt delivery of supplies from his Midland Terminal Railroad.

Then at 2:15 A.M. on June 6, 1904, an explosion ripped through the platform of the Independence train depot. Twenty-five non-union miners from A. E. Carlton's Findley Mine were at the train depot. Thirteen men were killed and several were wounded or otherwise mutilated.

The MOA and the Citizens Alliance demanded an end to the strike and those responsible for the explosion prosecuted. In the end, compromise was exercised on both sides and the strike ended.

Sheriff Edward Bell, brother of Sherman Bell, and his men escorted a group of union sympathizers to the train station where they were loaded onto freight cars with orders to never come back to the district. Emma Langdon was one of those forced out of town.

When Emma arrived in Denver, she decided to stay. Here she continued her work for Colorado labor causes and was a founding member of the Industrial Workers of the World in 1905. In 1913, Emma helped unite typographical union members in Colorado, New Mexico, and Wyoming.

Emma Langdon died on November 29, 1937, at age sixty-two. She was buried in a vault in Denver's Fairmont Cemetery, alongside her daughter.

Emma Langdon single-handedly kept a newspaper in print during a violent labor strike and continued to work tirelessly for the average worker.

Katy Bemore: Eyewitness to History

When Katy Bemore moved to the mining town of Independence in the Cripple Creek Mining District in 1898, she had no idea the events she would witness.

Frank and twenty-six-year-old Katy Bemore, along with their four children, arrived in Independence from Kansas. Independence was a thriving mining community, and

Frank quickly found employment. People were constantly moving to Independence due to the vast employment opportunities at W. S. Stratton's Independence Mine. At the height of production, more than 1,100 men worked at the mine.

Due to housing shortages, Frank and Katy bought the engine shack and hoist room of an abandoned mine. Apparently, the mine had flooded from underground water. In time, the shaft became a well and at a time when people paid by the bucket for water piped in from nearby Altman, this became a godsend to residents. Frank and a few friends erected a pulley with a bucket. Katy used to watch people come to the waterhole from her front window.

Over time, Frank added to Katy's little shack when he could afford the lumber. The town featured grocery stores, meat markets, a mercantile, clothing stores, saloons, and doctors' offices. The Bemore children attended school at the two-story schoolhouse at Independence. Sadly, their youngest child, Daisy, died after graduating from the eighth grade.

Shortly after her arrival, Katy witnessed the first run of the Florence and Cripple Creek Railroad. It must have been a thrill to witness such progress at such an exciting time.

Then Katy's world was rocked by an explosion. At 2:15 A.M. on June 6, 1904, Katy was awakened by a blast. Katy later said, "It lifted the bed right off the floor."[14] Frank quickly dressed and rushed to the scene. Katy soon followed.

The blast occurred at the Florence and Cripple Creek Railroad depot, nearly destroying the building. This was during the violent labor war of 1903–1904. It was soon determined that the explosion was set by members of the labor union. Thirteen men were dead. Others were horribly maimed or wounded. Katy later recalled, "Boots, parts of clothing and bodies lay everywhere. There was no way to identify the dead."[15]

Katy watched as officials stretched a rope barrier around the scene and then began the gruesome task of picking up pieces of the remains of the thirteen miners.

Not long after this, Frank quit mining and opened a lunch counter service in Victor. Katy took the trolley to Victor every day and did the cooking. On Christmas Day 1909, Frank Bemore suddenly died. Katy was left to run the lunch counter on her own. She had $8 to her name after burying her husband.

Katy Bemore spent the next fifty years in her little mining shack, comfortable in her surroundings and her memories. She died peacefully on March 25, 1963, and was buried in Evergreen Cemetery in Colorado Springs. Katy Bemore was ninety-one years old.

Notes

1. Levine, Brian. *Cripple Creek Gold: A Centennial History of the Cripple Creek District.* The Depot, 1988. p. 50.
2. Hills, Fred. *The Official Manual: Cripple Creek District.* Fred Hills, 1900. p. 58.
3. ibid., p. 83.
4. Levine, *Cripple Creek Gold,* p. 53.
5. ibid.
6. *Cripple Creek City Directory.*
7. Obituary, *Gazette Telegraph,* Monday, December 15, 1958.
8. *Cripple Creek Business Directory,* 1900.
9. *Colorado Springs Gazette,* December 15, 1901.
10. Spencer Penrose Collection, Box 55, File 243. Penrose House, Colorado Springs.
11 Obituary, *Gazette Telegraph,* Monday, December 15, 1958.
12. Taylor, Robert G. *Cripple Creek Mining District.* Filter Press, 1973. p. 97.
13. Jameson, Elizabeth. *All That Glitters: Class, Conflict, and Community.* University of Illinois Press, 1998. p. 215.
14. Interview in the *Cripple Creek Gold Rush,* May 30, 1952.
15. ibid.

EPILOGUE

WOMEN ARE INVOLVED IN MINING TO THIS DAY. Several Colorado mining corporations routinely hire women miners, including Climax, Argo, and the state's largest mining company, the Cripple Creek Victor Mining Company or Newmont Mining. Women also work in the mining industry as scientists, biologists, and chemists.

The legacy of women miners continues on.

BIBLIOGRAPHY

Government Publications

Colorado, Adjutant General's Office. *Ludlow: Being the Report of the Special Board of Officers Appointed by the Governor of Colorado to Investigate and Determine the Facts with Reference to the Armed Conflict Between the Colorado National Guard and Certain Persons Engaged in the Coal Mining Strike at Ludlow, Colo., April 20, 1914.* Williamson-Haffner Co., Denver, Colorado, 1914.

Ludlow Tent Colony Site. United States Department of the Interior, National Park Service National Register of Historic Places Registration Form.

Report of West Virginia Mining Investigation Commission, August 28, 1913.

The Colorado Coal Miner's Strike: Industrial Relations: Final Report and Testimony Submitted to Congress. Washington, D.C., U.S. Government Printing Office, 1916.

State and Federal Documental Archives and Sources.

Colorado State Division of Vital Statistics.

The National Archives and Records Administration, Denver Federal Center.

Unpublished Works and Manuscripts.

McGovern, George S. "The Colorado Coal Strike, 1913–1914." PhD dissertation, Northwestern University, Evanston, Illinois, 1953.

Newspapers

The various local newspaper archives accessed for this work are noted in the specific quotes used throughout the text.

Historical Archives and Resources

Argo Tunnel and Mill, Idaho Springs, CO.

Augusta Tabor files. Western History Department, Denver Public Library.

Colorado College
Tutt Library collections.

Colorado History Center
William N. Byers Papers.
CCWAP (Colorado Coalfield War Archaeological Project), 2000.
Investigations into the Ludlow Massacre Site, 1998.
Laura Evans taped interviews conducted by her lawyer, Fred Mazzulla, held at History Center Colorado.

Denver Public Library Western History Collection.

Rocky Mountain News Archives.

Thayer, William M. *Marvels of the New West.* The Henry Bill Publishing Company, 1886. Courtesy Denver Public Library, Western History Research Room.

Historical Society of Idaho Springs.

University of Denver

Gray, Anna. "Contested Ideals: Cultural Citizenship at the Ludlow Tent Colony." Master's thesis, University of Denver, 2005.

Project #03-02-020, Product 4. Colorado Coalfield War Archaeological Project, Department of Anthropology, University of Denver, n.d. Larkin, Karin, Mark Walker, Michael Jacobson, and Anna Gray, with contributions by Dean Saitta, Randall McGuire, Andrea Zlotucha Kozub, April Beisaw, and Erin Saar, Denver, Colorado.

Archaeological Investigations at the Ludlow Massacre Site (5LA1829) and Berwind CF&I Coal Camp (5LA2175), Las Animas County, Colorado: Final Synthetic Report, Denver, CO: Colorado Coalfield War Archaeological Project, Department of Anthropology, University of Denver, 1 September 2005.

Testimonies and Memories: Voices From the Ludlow Massacre Survive. Denver University Library Archives.

Primary Sources

Thomas, Mary. *Those Damn Foreigners.* Minerva Books, 1971.
Jolly, Pearl. *Under Fire in the Ludlow Tent Colony.* Self-published, 1916.

Penrose Collection, Penrose House, Colorado Springs.

Periodicals and Historical Journals.

True Story Magazine, 1937. A four-part series titled "Baby Doe Tabor," by Sue Bonnie. This was actually commissioned and written by Caroline Bancroft.

Books

Atkinson, Linda. *The Most Dangerous Woman in America.* Crown Publishing, 1978.

Backus, Harriet Fish. *Tomboy Bride.* Pruett Publishing, 1969.

Baker, Roger. *Clara: An Ex-slave in Gold Rush Colorado.* Black Hawk Publishing Co. 2003.

Bancroft, Caroline. *Gulch of Gold.* Johnson Publishing, 1958.

BIBLIOGRAPHY

Bancroft, Caroline. *Silver Queen; The Fabulous Story of Baby Doe Tabor.* Johnson Books, 1953.

Beach, Tracy. *My Life as a Whore: The Biography of Madam Laura Evans.* Johnson Books, 2015.

Beardsley, Isaac Haight. *Echoes From Peak and Plain.* Curtis & Jennings, 1898.

Beaton, Gail. *Colorado Women: A History.* University Press of Colorado, 2012.

Beebe, Lucius and Clegg, Charles. *Narrow Gauge in the Rockies.* Howell-North Publishers, 1958.

Blair, Edward. *Leadville: Colorado's Magic City.* Pruett Publishing, 1980.

Bradley, Christine A. and Smith, Duane A. *The Once and Future Silver Queen of the Rockies.* University Press of Colorado, 2019.

Chernow, Ron. *Titan: The Life of John D. Rockefeller Sr.* Random House, 1998.

Clyne, Rick J. *Coal People: Life in Southern Colorado's Company Towns, 1890–1930.* Colorado History Center, 1999.

Crum, Josie Moore. *Rails Among the Peaks.* Railroading Printing House, 1956.

Ellis, Amanda M. *Bonanza Towns: Leadville and Cripple Creek.* J.D. Simpson & Company, 1954.

Enss, Chris. *A Beautiful Mine: Women Prospectors of the Old West.* TwoDot Publishers, 2008.

Gitelman, H. M. *Legacy of the Ludlow Massacre: A Chapter in American Industrial Relations.* University of Pennsylvania Press, 1988.

Graham, John. "Introduction," in *The Coal War.* Edited by Upton Sinclair. Boulder, CO. Associated University Press, 1976.

Guerin, E. J. *Mountain Charley or the Adventures of Mrs. E. J. Guerin, Who Was Thirteen Years in Male Attire.* Self-published, Dubuque, Iowa, 1861. Reprinted by University of Oklahoma Press, 1968.

Hargraves, Orin. *The Fabulous Life of Angeline Louisiana Munn.* Self-published, 2019.

Hills, Fred. *The Official Manual of the Cripple Creek District.* Fred Hills, Publisher, 1900.

Historical Society of Idaho Springs. *History of Clear Creek County, and the Families Who Shaped Colorado's Premier Mining District.* Historical Society of Idaho Springs, 1986.

Iversen, Kristen. *Molly Brown: Unraveling the Myth.* Johnson Books, 1999.

Jameson, Elizabeth. *All That Glitters: Class, Conflict, and Community in Cripple Creek.* University of Illinois Press, 1998.

Jessen, Kenneth. *Georgetown: A Quick History.* First Light Publishing, 1996.

Levine, Brian. *Cripple Creek: City of Influence, Historic Preservation of Cripple Creek.* 1994.

Levine, Brian. *Cripple Creek Gold.* The Depot, 1988.

Leyendecker, Liston E. *The Griffith Family & the Founding of Georgetown.* University Press of Colorado, 2001.

Lohse, Joyce B. *Baby Doe Tabor: Matchless Silver Queen.* Filter Press, 2011.

Marshall, Thomas M. *Early Records of Gilpin County 1859-1861.* University of Colorado, 1920.

McClenny, Laura. *Women of the Upper Rio Grande: Beartown to Creede.* Downing Company Publishers, 2011.

McLean, Evalyn Walsh. *Father Struck It Rich.* Bear Creek Publishing, 1936.

Montoya, Fawn-Amber and Larkin, Karin, editors. *Communities of Ludlow.* University Press of Colorado, 2022.

Moynihan, Betty. *Augusta Tabor: A Pioneering Woman.* Cordillera Press, Inc., 1988.

Noel, Thomas J. *Denver, Rocky Mountain Gold.* The Denver Chamber of Commerce, 1980.

Noel, Thomas J. and Norman, Cathleen M. *A Pikes Peak Partnership: The Penroses and the Tutts.* University Press of Colorado, 2000.

O. L. Baskins. *History of Boulder and Clear Creek Counties.* O. L. Baskins & Company, 1880, reprinted 1973.

O'Neal, Papanikolas Zeese. *Buried Unsung: Louis Tikas and the Ludlow Massacre.* University of Utah Press, 1982.

Parkill, Forbes. *Wildest of the West.* Henry Holt and Company, 1951.

Royem, Robert T. *America's Railroad: Durango & Silverton Narrow Gauge Railroad.* Durango & Silverton Narrow Gauge Railroad Company, 2007.

Ruby, Lois. *Strike! Mother Jones & the Colorado Coal Field War.* Filter Press, LLC, 2012.

Shirley, Gayle C. and Wommack, Linda. *Remarkable Colorado Women.* TwoDot Publishers, 2023.

Smith, Duane A. *San Juan Bonanza.* University of New Mexico Press, 2006.

Smith, Duane A. *San Juan Legacy.* University of New Mexico Press, 2009.

Smith, Duane A. *Rocky Mountain Mining Camps.* University Press of Colorado, 1992.

Sprague, Marshall. *Money Mountain.* University of Nebraska Press, 1953.

Steel, Edward. *The Correspondence of Mother Jones.* University of Pittsburgh Press, 1985.

Stewart, John. *Thomas F. Walsh: Progressive Businessman and Colorado Mining Tycoon.* University of Colorado Press, 2007.

Taylor, Robert Guilford. *Cripple Creek Mining District.* Filter Press, 1973.

Thomas, Mary. *Those Damn Foreigners.* Minerva Books, 1971.

Tucker, E. F. *Otto Mears and the San Juans.* Western Reflections Publishing, 2003.

Varnell, Jeanne. *Women of Consequence.* Johnson Books, 1999.

Voynick, Stephen M. *Leadville: A Miner's Epic.* Mountain Press Publishing, 1984.

Whitacre, Christine. *Molly Brown: Denver's Unsinkable Lady.* Historic Denver, Inc., 1988.

Wommack, Linda. *Cripple Creek, Bob Womack and the Greatest Gold Camp on Earth.* Rhyolite Press, 2019.

Wommack, Linda. *From the Grave: A Roadside Guide to Colorado's Pioneer Cemeteries.* Caxton Press, 1998.

Wommack, Linda. *Our Ladies of the Tenderloin: Colorado's Legends in Lace.* Caxton Press, 2005.

INDEX

Page numbers in **bold** indicate photos.

INDEX

INDEX

INDEX

ABOUT THE AUTHOR

A **COLORADO NATIVE, LINDA WOMMACK** is a Colorado historian and historical consultant. An award-winning writer, she has written eighteen books on Colorado history, including *Murder in the Mile High City, Colorado's Landmark Hotels, From the Grave: A Roadside Guide to Colorado's Pioneer Cemeteries, Our Ladies of the Tenderloin: Colorado's Legends in Lace, Colorado History for Kids, Colorado's Historic Mansions and Castles, Colorado's Historic Schools, Ann Bassett: Colorado's Cattle Queen, Haunted History of Cripple Creek and Teller County, Growing Up with the Wild Bunch, Ranching Women of Colorado, Cripple Creek, Bob Womack and the Greatest Gold Camp on Earth,* and *From Sand Creek to Summit Springs: Colorado's Indian Wars.* She has also contributed to two anthologies concerning Western Americana. She is a three-time winner of the prestigious Will Rogers Medallion Award.

Linda has been a contributing editor for *True West Magazine* since 1995 and has been a staff writer for *Wild West* magazine, contributing a monthly article since 2004. She has written for the *Tombstone Epitaph,* the nation's oldest continuously published newspaper, since 1993. Linda also writes for several publications throughout her state and has won two awards for her work.

Linda's research has been used in several documentary accounts for the national Wild West History Association, historical treatises of the Sand Creek Massacre, and as critical historical aspects for the Lawman & Outlaw Museum as well as the Heritage Center, both in Cripple Creek, Colorado.

Linda is a member of both the state and national Cemetery Preservation Associations, the Gilpin County Historical Society, the national Wild West History Association, and is an honorary lifetime member of the Pikes Peak Heritage Society. As a member of Women Writing the West, Linda has organized quarterly meetings for Colorado members of WWW for the past ten years, served on the 2014 and 2020 WWW conference steering committees, and recently concluded her term as a board member. Linda is the chair for the Women Writing the West DOWNING Journalism Award, an award category she created for the organization in 2017.

Linda won the Will Rogers Medallion Award for Best Biography for *Ann Bassett* and *Growing Up With the Wild Bunch,* and Best Non-Fiction for *Ranching Women of Colorado.* She has received the Six-Shooter Award twice for her magazine articles, "Confidentially Told in Brown's Park" and "In the Shadow of Tom Horn." In 2023, Linda was inducted into the Colorado Authors Hall of Fame.